Index to the Probate Court Records

of

Sonoma County, California

1847–1879

Steven M. Lovejoy

HERITAGE BOOKS
2020

HERITAGE BOOKS
AN IMPRINT OF HERITAGE BOOKS, INC.

Books, CDs, and more—Worldwide

For our listing of thousands of titles see our website
at
www.HeritageBooks.com

Published 2020 by
HERITAGE BOOKS, INC.
Publishing Division
5810 Ruatan Street
Berwyn Heights, Md. 20740

Cover image: Sonoma County, California, Probate Court Minute Book G: 437,
estates of John and Joseph Lewis, minors, 4 June 1869;
Sonoma County Archives, Santa Rosa, California.

Heritage Books by the author:

Guide to the Court of Sessions Records of Sonoma County, California, 1850–1863
Index to the Probate Court Records of Sonoma County, California, 1847–1879
Index to the Public Official Bonds of Sonoma County, California, 1850–1892

International Standard Book Number
Paperbound: 978-0-7884-0417-7

Table of Contents

Introduction

The Probate Court of Sonoma County officially existed from 1 May 1851 through 31 December 1879 and handled all matters pertaining to the disposition of deceased persons' estates and the guardianship of minors and insane or incompetent persons. The records of the courts which dealt with these matters before the Probate Court was established, the Alcalde Court of Sonoma District and the County Court of Sonoma County, are included in the records of the Probate Court of Sonoma County. On 1 January 1880, the jurisdiction over probate matters in Sonoma County was transferred to the newly established Superior Court of Sonoma County.

In 2014 the Sonoma County Genealogical Society published a two-volume transcription of the first several volumes of Sonoma County's general probate index, 1847 to 1959.[1] Each entry in this publication indicates the individual's name, the probate case file number, the type of probate case involved (deceased person's estate, minor's guardianship, or insane/incompetent person's guardianship), and a date (or year or range of years). Knowing the probate case file number researchers can locate the probate case file containing all of the papers filed in the case housed at the Sonoma County Superior Court.

To fully understand how a probate case unfolded over time, however, in addition to the filed documents in the probate case file both the fee book and registers and minute books of the court which handled the probate case need to be consulted. Unfortunately, for most courts, these bound volumes are usually unindexed, requiring tedious page-by-page searches for information about each probate case. This publication assists researchers by providing an index to both the fee book and registers and minute books of the Probate Court of Sonoma County, 1847–1879. It includes Sonoma County probate case file numbers 1 through 1056 and comprises over 1,400 individual entries.

Researchers should use this index to locate the appropriate entries in the Sonoma County Probate Court fee book and registers and minute books to reconstruct the proceedings of the probate case and examine each and every document in an individual's probate case file. In addition, any other documents which may be mentioned in these bound volumes but not included in an individual's probate case file, such as wills and/or guardianship bonds, should be located and examined.[2] For probate cases still pending in the Probate Court at the end of 1879 researchers should examine the records of the Superior Court for further proceedings.

---

[1] Sonoma County Genealogical Society, *Probate Records, Sonoma County, California, Index for 1847 to 1959, Volume 1: A–K* (Berwyn Heights, Maryland: Heritage Books, Inc., 2014) and *Probate Records, Sonoma County, California, Index for 1847 to 1959, Volume 2: L–Z* (Berwyn Heights, Maryland: Heritage Books, Inc., 2014).
[2] See, Sonoma County Genealogical Society, *Index and Abstracts of Wills, Sonoma County, California, 1850–1900* (Westminster, Maryland: Heritage Books, Inc., 2007) and Sonoma County Genealogical Society, compiler, *Bonds of Guardianship* (Santa Rosa, California: Sonoma County Genealogical Society, no date).

How to Use this Index

This index to the records of the Probate Court of Sonoma County is presented in a five-column tabular form. The first column, **Name**, which is arranged alphabetically by surname, gives the name or names associated with each probate case file. These are names of deceased persons leaving estates which require disposition and minors and insane or incompetent persons needing guardians appointed to manage their affairs. Deceased persons' probate case files sometimes include documents concerning the guardianship of their minor children, and so the probate case file number for both the deceased person's estate and their minor children's guardianship will be the same. At other times, there will be separate probate case files.

Spelling in the 19th century was not standardized. Names, especially surnames, can be spelled a variety of ways on documents within each probate case. Name variations are indicated by a slash (/) between variations. For example, Bedwell/Bidwell indicates both forms of the surname, Bedwell and Bidwell, are found in the records. Researchers are advised to look for all possible variations of a name for which they are searching.

The second column, **File #**, gives the probate case file number (1 through 1056) which can be used to locate the documents filed in each probate case. Both the Sonoma County Superior Court Archived Records Division and the Probate Division hold these probate case files. The original documents in each probate case file were microfilmed and have recently been digitized. The fate of the original documents is unknown. Probate case file numbers 428 and 874 were not used.

The third column, **Type**, gives the type of probate case file for each individual's entry. D indicates a deceased person's case file, M indicates a minor's guardianship case file, and I indicates an insane or incompetent person's guardianship case file.

The fourth column, **Fee Book & Register**, gives the volume (or volumes) and page number (or numbers) on which each probate case was recorded in the four bound volumes of Sonoma County Probate Court fee book and registers. See the Records Utilized section for detailed descriptions of each of these four registers.

The fifth column, **Minute Book**, gives the volume (or volumes) and page number (or numbers) on which each probate case was recorded in the existing fourteen Sonoma County Probate Court minute books. See the Records Utilized section for detailed descriptions of each of these fourteen books.

Records Utilized

1. Sonoma County Probate Court fee book and registers

The fee book and registers record the papers filed and court actions taken in each probate case along with the associated costs. They are "probably the most important of the court records, as they contain in one place practically a full record of each case."[3] The four bound Sonoma County Probate Court fee book and registers listed below are housed in the Sonoma County Archives.[4]

a. Book A, probate case numbers 1 through 148, dated 3 August 1847 through 30 September 1859, 204 stamped pages, only pages 1–163 are written on, indexed, Sonoma County Archives accession # 1371.

b. Book B, probate case numbers 76 through 407, dated 4 October 1859 through 1 March 1869, 851 stamped pages, pages 1, 2, 72, and 732 are blank, indexed, Sonoma County Archives accession # 1372.

c. Book C, probate case numbers 408 through 764, dated 15 March 1869 through 7 September 1875, 800 stamped pages, pages 1 and 800 are blank, no index, Sonoma County Archives accession # 1373.

d. Book D, probate case numbers 765 through 1056, dated 9 September 1875 through 30 December 1879, 601 stamped pages, pages 597–600 are torn out, pages 304–601 are blank, indexed, Sonoma County Archives accession # 1374.

2. Sonoma County Probate Court minute books

The minute books record the day-to-day proceedings of the Probate Court and contain a synopsis of all orders, judgments, and decrees in each probate case. The fourteen bound Sonoma County Probate Court minute books listed below are housed in the Sonoma County Archives. Digital images of minute books D through O below are also available for free on *FamilySearch* (https://www.familysearch.org). The Probate Court minute book containing minutes from May 1850 through April 1854 (presumably entitled Book A) which was in the vault of the County Clerk when the inventory of the records of the Sonoma County Clerk's Office was conducted in 1979–80 is now missing, misplaced, or misshelved.[5]

---

[3] Owen C. Coy, *Guide to the County Archives of California* (Sacramento, California: California Historical Survey Commission, 1919), 24.

[4] The Sonoma County Archives are managed by the Sonoma County Library. Contact the Sonoma County History and Genealogy Library, 725 3rd Street, Santa Rosa, CA 95404, (707) 308-3212, history@sonomalibrary.com, to request access to the Sonoma County Probate Court bound volumes.

[5] Sonoma County Records Inventory Project, *Inventory of Records, 1847-1980, Office the Clerk, Sonoma County, California* (Rohnert Park, California: Reference Department, Ruben Salazar Library, Sonoma State University, 1982), 105. This volume is inventory number 269.

a. Book B, entries are dated 24 April 1854 through 18 August 1857, 430 total pages (429 stamped pages, page 430 is handwritten), pages 1–54 are an alphabetical index, but this is entirely blank except for one entry under the letter K (Kelsey, Jos. & Wm., p. 109, 112, 116, 130, 141), minutes begin on page 55, Sonoma County Archives accession # 2663.

b. Book C, entries are dated 1 September 1857 through 3 October 1857, 395 stamped pages, only pages 1–11 are written on, no index, Sonoma County Archives accession # 2662.

c. Book D, entries are dated 5 October 1857 through 6 June 1859, 380 pages, pages 1–22 are blank, separate index, Sonoma County Archives accession # 1300.

d. Book E, entries are dated 10 June 1859 through 21 November 1862, 637 stamped pages, pages 21–24 are missing, pages 144, 598, and 633–637 are blank, no index, Sonoma County Archives accession # 1301.

e. Book F, entries are dated 1 December 1862 through 24 December 1866, 802 stamped pages, pages 130, 131, 140, and 141 are torn out, pages 1 and 210 are blank, no index, Sonoma County Archives accession # 1302.

f. Book G, entries are dated 3 January 1867 through 28 March 1870, 656 stamped pages, no index, Sonoma County Archives accession # 1303.

g. Book H, entries are dated 4 April 1870 through 5 March 1872, 600 stamped pages, pages 599–600 are blank, no index, Sonoma County Archives accession # 1304.

h. Book I, entries are dated 11 March 1872 through 21 May 1873, 600 stamped pages, pages 49–50 are cut off (note on what's left of page 49: "An awkward fellow upset a bottle of ink on this page, thereby marring its beautiful appearance, and consequently, like all things defiled, had to be cut off and cast away."), pages 594–600 are blank, no index, Sonoma County Archives accession # 1305.

i. Book J, entries are dated 26 May 1873 through 15 December 1874, 640 stamped pages, no index, Sonoma County Archives accession # 1306.

j. Book K, entries are dated 17 December 1874 through 31 December 1875, 480 stamped pages, pages 463–480 are blank, no index, last line reads: "Here endeth, for the present, the Judicial administration of the Hon. A. P. Overton. R.I.P.," Sonoma County Archives accession # 1307.

k. Book L, entries are dated 3 January 1876 through 29 January 1877, 641 stamped pages, page 641 is blank, no index, Sonoma County Archives accession # 1308.

l. Book M, entries are dated 29 January 1877 through 14 December 1877, 640 stamped pages, pages 173–174 are cut out, no index, Sonoma County Archives accession # 1309.

m. Book N, entries are dated 14 December 1877 through 24 December 1878, 641 stamped pages, pages 638 and 641 are blank, pages 639–640 are cut out, no index, Sonoma County Archives accession # 1310.

n. Book O, entries are dated 30 December 1878 through 31 December 1879, 640 stamped pages, pages 534–640 are blank, no index, Sonoma County Archives accession # 1311.

History of the Probate Court of Sonoma County

Prior to the creation of the Probate Court of Sonoma County in 1851 probate matters in the area now called Sonoma County were handled by the Alcalde Court of the District of Sonoma and then for about a year by the County Court of Sonoma County. The first six probate cases one now finds included among the records of the Probate Court of Sonoma County, in fact, originated in the Alcalde Court and are dated from 1847 to 1849.

The Alcalde judicial system was replaced in 1849 when the first constitution of California was ratified. This constitution established a new judicial system whose powers were vested in a supreme court, district courts, county courts, and justices of the peace.[6] The county court was to be presided over by a county judge who was to "perform the duties of Surrogate, or Probate Judge."[7] The California legislature delineated the procedures of the county court on 13 April 1850 when it passed "An Act to organize the County Courts," which directed the county judge to hold a term of the court for the transacting of probate business on the first Monday of each month.[8] The procedures for transacting this probate business were laid out in an act passed nine days later.[9]

On 11 March 1851, the California legislature sitting at its second session passed "An Act Concerning the Courts of Justice of this State, and Judicial Officers," which created among other courts a separate probate court in each California county and conferred upon it its jurisdiction.[10] The county judge was to be the judge of the probate court, and he was directed to hold this court on the fourth Monday of each month (except San Francisco County).[11] The probate court was to have exclusive jurisdiction, in the first instance, to take proof of wills in five specific situations. It was also to have jurisdiction to:

> 1.) take proof of a will relative to real property, situated in the county when the testator shall have died outside of California, not being an inhabitant thereof, and not leaving assets therein,

---

[6] Constitution of the State of California, 1849, Article VI (Judicial Department), section 1.

[7] Constitution of the State of California, 1849, Article VI (Judicial Department), section 8.

[8] *The Statutes of California, Passed at the First Session of the Legislature, Begun the 15th Day of Dec. 1849, and Ended the 22nd Day of April, 1850, at the City of Pueblo de San José* (San José: J. Winchester, State Printer, 1850), pp. 217–218, Chap. 92, "An Act to organize the County Courts" (hereinafter cited as *The Statutes of California, First Session*).

[9] *The Statutes of California, First Session*, pp. 377–404, Chap. 129, "An Act to regulate the Settlement of the Estates of Deceased Persons." This act was passed on 22 April 1850.

[10] *The Statutes of California, Passed at the Second Session of the Legislature: Begun on the Sixth Day of January, 1851, and Ended on the First Day of May, 1851, at the City of San Jose* (n.p.: Eugene Casserly, State Printer, 1851), pp. 9–31, Chap. 1, "An Act Concerning the Courts of Justice of this State, and Judicial Officers," specifically pp. 21–22, § 78 through § 85 (hereinafter cited as *The Statutes of California, Second Session*). This act was passed on 11 March 1851, but it was to take effect on 1 May 1851.

[11] *The Statutes of California, Second Session*, pp. 31–34, Chap. 2, "An Act Amending an Act entitled, 'An Act Concerning the Courts of Justice of this State, and Judicial Officers'," specifically p. 34, § 9.

2.) grant and revoke letters testamentary and of administration,

3.) direct and control the conduct and settle the accounts of executors and administrators,

4.) enforce the payments of debts and legacies, and the distribution of the estates of intestates,

5.) order the sale and disposal of the real property of deceased persons,

6.) take the care and custody of the person and estate of an infant residing in the county, and of the person and estate of an individual residing in the county, who from any cause is incapable of taking care of himself and of managing his property, and

7.) appoint and remove guardians, to direct and control their conduct, and to settle their accounts.

In 1853 the California legislature repealed the Court Act of 1851 and replaced it with an act of the same name.[12] The county judge was still to be the judge of the probate court, and he was still to hold this court on the fourth Monday of every month (except in San Francisco County). The jurisdiction of the probate court was, however, amended to:

1.) open and receive the proof of last wills and testaments, and to admit them to probate,

2.) grant letters testamentary, of administration, and of guardianship, and to revoke the same, for cause shown according to law,

3.) compel executors, administrators, and guardians to render an account when required, or at the period fixed by law,

4.) order the sale of property of estates or belonging to minors,

5.) order the payment of debts due by estates,

6.) order and regulate all partitions of property or estate of deceased persons,

7.) compel the attendance of witnesses,

8.) appoint appraisers or arbitrators,

---

[12] *The Statutes of California, Passed at the Fourth Session of the Legislature, Begun on the Third of January, 1853, and Ended on the Nineteenth Day of May, 1853, at the Cities of Vallejo and Benicia* (San Francisco: George Kerr, State Printer, 1853), pp. 287–305, Chap. CLXXX, "An Act Concerning the Courts of Justice of this State, and Judicial Officers," specifically pp. 297–298, sec. 61 through sec. 65 (hereinafter cited as *The Statutes of California, Fourth Session*). This act was approved 19 May 1853, but it was to take effect on 6 June 1853.

9.) compel the production of title deeds, papers, or other property of an estate or of a minor, and

10.) make such other orders, as may be necessary and proper, in the exercise of the jurisdiction conferred upon the Probate Court.

In an act approved by the California legislature on 9 April 1856 the courts authorized to be held by the county judge of Sonoma County, which included the probate court, were to be held on the first Mondays of January, April, July, and October.[13] In 1859 the beginning term dates for the probate court of Sonoma county were changed to the first Mondays of February, May, August, and November.[14]

In 1863 the California legislature repealed the Court Act of 1853 and again replaced it with an act of the same name.[15] The county judge remained the judge of probate (except in the city and county of San Francisco), and the jurisdiction of the probate court was unchanged. The beginnings of the terms of the probate court were amended to "at such times as may be provided by law." For Sonoma County these dates remained the first Mondays of February, May, August, and November.

In 1866 an act by the California legislature again changed the beginnings of the terms of the probate court of Sonoma County to the first Monday of every month.[16] These beginning dates remained so through two subsequent amendatory acts in 1868 and 1872.[17] When the Code of

---

[13] *The Statutes of California, Passed at the Seventh Session of the Legislature, Begun on the Seventh Day of January, One Thousand Eight Hundred and Fifty-six, and Ended on the Twenty-first Day of April, One Thousand Eight Hundred and Fifty-six, at the City of Sacramento* (Sacramento: James Allen, State Printer, 1856), p. 117, Chap. XCIX, "An Act Fixing the Time of Holding the Several Courts Authorized to be Held by the County Judge in the County of Sonoma."

[14] *The Statutes of California, Passed at the Tenth Session of the Legislature, Begun on Monday, the Third Day of January, and Ended on Tuesday, the Nineteenth Day of April* (Sacramento: John O'Meara, State Printer, 1859), pp. 225–226, Chap. CCXIX, "An Act fixing the Terms of the County Court, Probate Court, and Court of Sessions, in Counties therein named."

[15] *The Statutes of California, Passed at the Fourteenth Session of the Legislature, 1863: Begun on Monday, the Fifth Day of January, and Ended on Monday, the Twenty-seventh Day of April* (Sacramento: Benj. P. Avery, State Printer, 1863), pp. 333–346, Chap. CCLX, "An Act Concerning the Courts of Justice of this State, and Judicial Officers," specifically pp. 338–339, sec. 42 through sec. 46 (hereinafter cited as *The Statutes of California, Fourteenth Session*). This act was approved on 20 April 1863, but it was to take effect on 1 January 1864.

[16] *The Statutes of California, Passed at the Sixteenth Session of the Legislature, 1865–6, Began on Monday, the Fourth Day of December, Eighteen Hundred and Sixty-five, and Ended on Monday, the Second Day of April, Eighteen Hundred and Sixty-six* (Sacramento: O. M. Clayes, State Printer, 1866), p. 198, Chap. CCIV, "An Act to fix the terms of the County Court and Probate Court of the County of Sonoma."

[17] *The Statutes of California, Passed at the Seventeenth Session of the Legislature, 1867–8, Began on Monday, the Second Day of December, Eighteen Hundred and Sixty-seven, and Ended on Monday, the Thirtieth Day of March, Eighteen Hundred and Sixty-eight* (Sacramento: D. W. Gelwicks, State Printer, 1868), pp. 537–538, Chap. CCCCXXI, "An Act to amend an Act to fix the terms of the County Court and Probate Court of the County of Sonoma, approved March tenth, eighteen hundred and sixty-six." *The Statutes of California, Passed at the Nineteenth Session of the Legislature, 1871–72, Began on Monday, the Fourth Day of December, Eighteen Hundred and Seventy-one, and Ended on Monday, the First Day of April, Eighteen Hundred and Seventy-two* (Sacramento: T. A.

Civil Procedure was adopted in 1872 two small word changes were made to the jurisdiction of the probate court: 1.) the word "proof" was substituted for the word "probate" in the phrase "open and receive proof of last wills and testaments, and to admit them to probate" and 2.) the word "distributions" was substituted for the word "partitions" in the phrase "order and regulate all partitions of property or estates of deceased persons."[18] Finally, in 1878 the beginning dates of the terms of the probate court of Sonoma County were changed back to the first Mondays of January, April, July, and October as they were in 1856, amending section 99 of the Code of Civil Procedure.[19]

The probate courts were abolished when the second California constitution was ratified in 1879.[20] Section 1 of Article VI of this new constitution vested the judicial power of the State "in the Senate sitting as a Court of Impeachment, in a Supreme Court, Superior Courts, Justices of the Peace, and such inferior Courts as the Legislature may establish in any incorporated city or town, or city and county."[21] The Superior Court was to have original jurisdiction "in all matters of probate" and always be open.[22] "All records, books, papers, and proceedings" from the probate courts were to be transferred to the Superior Courts on 1 January 1880.[23]

Springer, State Printer, 1872), p. 844, Chap. DLXXIII, "An Act amendatory of an Act entitled an Act to amend an Act to fix the terms of the County Court and Probate Court of the County of Sonoma, approved March thirty, eighteen hundred and sixty-eight."

[18] Warren Olney, compiler, *The Code of Civil Procedure of the State of California* (San Francisco: Sumner Whitney and Co., 1872), 44–46, Part I (Of Courts of Justice), Title I (Of Their Organization, Jurisdiction, and Terms), Chap. VI, "Of the Probate Courts," § 94 through § 100, specifically p. 45, § 97.

[19] *Acts Amendatory of the Codes of California Passed at the Twenty-second Session of the Legislature, 1877–8. Began on Monday, December Third, Eighteen Hundred and Seventy-seven, and Ended on Monday, April First, Eighteen Hundred and Seventy-eight* (Sacramento: State Office, F. P. Thompson, Supt. State Printing, 1878), pp. 94–97, Chap. CCL, "An Act to regulate certain Acts in relation to the terms of the County and Probate Courts in certain counties, and to amend sections eighty-eight and ninety-nine of the Code of Civil Procedure."

[20] Constitution of the State of California, 1879, Article XXII (Schedule), section 3.

[21] Constitution of the State of California, 1879, Article VI (Judicial Department), section 1.

[22] Constitution of the State of California, 1879, Article VI (Judicial Department), section 5.

[23] Constitution of the State of California, 1879, Article XXII (Schedule), section 3. *The Statutes of California Passed at the Twenty-third Session of the Legislature, 1880. Began on Monday, January Fifth, and Ended on Friday, April Sixteenth, One Thousand Eight Hundred and Eighty* (Sacramento: State Office, J. D. Young, Supt. State Printing, 1880), pp. 2–4, Chap IV, "An Act to transfer the records, papers, and business of the Courts existing on the thirty-first day of December, eighteen hundred and seventy-nine, in this State, to the Courts now existing therein," specifically p. 3, sec. 2.

County Judges of Sonoma County, 1850–1879

Below is a list of the County Judges of Sonoma County who presided over the Sonoma County Probate Court from 1851 through 1879.

1. Henry A. Green (served 1850–1851) was elected on 1 April 1850 and took his oath of office on 9 April 1850.[24] He died on 11 July 1851 at Sonoma of "liver complaint."[25] Martin E. Cooke was appointed on 6 August 1851 by Governor John McDougal to fill the vacancy caused by the death of H. A. Green, but Cooke declined to accept.[26]

2. William O. King (served 1851) was appointed on 13 August 1851 by Governor John McDougal to fill the vacancy caused by H. A. Green's death.[27] He took his oath of office on 16 August 1851.[28]

3. Charles P. Wilkins (served 1851–1854) was elected on 3 September 1851.[29] He took his oath of office on 8 September 1851.[30] California Secretary of State records indicate that he resigned sometime before 13 September 1852 when Governor John Bigler appointed Phillip R. Thompson as the County Judge of Sonoma County.[31] Evidence suggests, however, that this appointment

---

[24] Sonoma County, California, oath of office for H. A. Green as County Judge, 9 April 1850; Sonoma County Archives, Santa Rosa.

[25] "Died," *The Daily Alta California* (San Francisco, California), 18 July 1851, p. 2, col. 6. The death notice reads: "At Sonoma, on the 11th last, of liver complaint, the Hon. H. A. Green, Judge of Sonoma county."

[26] California, "Record" (Dec., 1849–Oct. 30, 1857), entry for Martin E. Cooke as a County Judge of Sonoma County, p. 44, 6 August 1851; Secretary of State Records, F3680-1; California State Archives, Sacramento.

[27] California, "Record" (Dec., 1849–Oct. 30, 1857), entry for William O. King as a County Judge of Sonoma County, p. 44, 13 August 1851; Secretary of State Records, F3680-1; California State Archives, Sacramento.

[28] Sonoma County, California, oath of office for William O. King as County Judge, 16 August 1851; Sonoma County Archives, Santa Rosa.

[29] Sonoma County, California, certificate of election for Charles P. Wilkins as County Judge, 8 September 1851; Sonoma County Archives, Santa Rosa.

[30] Sonoma County, California, oath of office for Charles P. Wilkins as County Judge, 8 September 1851; Sonoma County Archives, Santa Rosa.

[31] California, "Executive Records" (Dec., 1849–July, 1876), entry for Phillip R. Thompson as a County Judge of Sonoma County, p. 208, 13 September 1852; Secretary of State Records, F3680-2; California State Archives, Sacramento. Another Secretary of State record gives the date of appointment of Thompson as County Judge of Sonoma County, vice Charles P. Wilkins, resigned, as 7 February 1854. See, California, "Record" (Dec., 1849–Oct. 30, 1857), entry for Philip R. Thompson as a County Judge of Sonoma County, p. 46, 7 February 1854; Secretary of State Records, F3680-1; California State Archives, Sacramento.

never took effect.[32] Wilkins committed suicide on 1 August 1864 in Santa Rosa "by cutting his throat with a razor."[33] He is buried in Santa Rosa Rural Cemetery.[34]

4. Frank W. Shattuck (served 1854–1855) was elected on 7 September 1853 and commissioned on 27 September 1853.[35] He resigned on 21 January 1855, effective 1 February 1855.[36] He died on 14 October 1893 in Petaluma "from a stroke of paralysis."[37] He is buried in Cypress Hill Memorial Park in Petaluma.[38]

5. John E. McNair (served 1855) was appointed by Governor John Bigler on 23 January 1855, vice Shattuck resigned, to take effect on 1 February 1855.[39] He took his oath of office on 30 January 1855.[40] He died on 6 May 1856 in San Francisco at the Tehama House of "pulmonary consumption."[41]

6. William Churchman (served 1855–1863) was elected on 5 September 1855 to fill the Shattuck vacancy.[42] He was elected again on 5 October 1857 for a full term and took his oath of office on

---

[32] C. P. Wilkins's name as County Judge appears consistently in the County Court minutes from 3 November 1851 through 2 January 1854. See, Sonoma County, California, County Court Minute Book (20 January 1851–2 January 1854): 3–22, minutes of the County Court, 3 November 1851 to 2 January 1854; Sonoma County History and Genealogy Library, Santa Rosa. Also, no letter of resignation from Wilkins to Governor Bigler has been found among the Governor's correspondence, C. P. Wilkins's signature as County Judge can be found on documents included in Sonoma County probate case files from September 1851 to February 1854 and on oaths of office for various Sonoma County public officials from September 1851 to November 1853, and Phillip R. Thompson's signature as County Judge appears on no known documents.

[33] "Death of Judge Wilkins," *The Sonoma County Democrat* (Santa Rosa, California), 6 August 1864, p. 2, col. 1. "Shocking Death of an Old Californian," *Daily Alta California* (San Francisco, California), 4 August 1864, p. 1, col. 1.

[34] Ancestry, *Find A Grave*, database with images (https://www.findagrave.com : accessed 22 November 2019), memorial 29345498, Charles P. Wilkins (1820–1864), Santa Rosa Rural Cemetery, Santa Rosa, Sonoma County, California; gravestone photograph by Pamela Fowler Sweeney.

[35] California, "Record" (Dec., 1849–Oct. 30, 1857), entry for Frank W. Shattuck as a County Judge of Sonoma County, p. 45, 7 September 1853; Secretary of State Records, F3680-1; California State Archives, Sacramento.

[36] Frank W. Shattuck to Hon. John Bigler, Governor, letter of resignation, 21 January 1855; Governor's Office Records (1849–1974), Resignations (1849–1941), F3672:186; California State Archives, Sacramento.

[37] "Death of Judge F. W. Shattuck," *The Sonoma Democrat* (Santa Rosa, California), 21 October 1893, p. 1, col. 1. "Called Suddenly," *The Morning Call* (San Francisco, California), 15 October 1893, p. 9, col. 4.

[38] Ancestry, *Find A Grave*, database with images (https://www.findagrave.com : accessed 22 November 2019), memorial 74789772, Judge Francis William "Frank" Shattuck (1827–1893), Cypress Hill Memorial Park, Petaluma, Sonoma County, California; gravestone photograph by Marion.

[39] California, appointment of John E. McNair as County Judge of Sonoma County, 23 January 1855; Sonoma County Archives, Santa Rosa.

[40] Sonoma County, California, oath of office for John E. McNair as County Judge, 30 January 1855; Sonoma County Archives, Santa Rosa.

[41] "Died," *The Wide West* (San Francisco, California), 11 May 1856, p. 2, col. 7. The death notice reads: "In this city [San Francisco], May 6, of pulmonary consumption, Hon. John E. McNair, aged 26 years and 11 months." "Judge J. E. McNair," *The Petaluma (California) Weekly Journal and Sonoma County Advertiser*, 10 May 1856, p. 2, col. 2.

[42] "Official Vote of Sonoma County," *The Petaluma (California) Weekly Journal and Sonoma County Advertiser*, 29 September 1855, p. 2, col. 4.

30 March 1858.[43] He was once more elected on 7 September 1859 and took his oath of office on 3 October 1859.[44] He died on 4 November 1873 in Santa Rosa and is buried in Santa Rosa Rural Cemetery.[45]

7. Charles Wadsworth Langdon (served 1864–1871) was elected on 21 October 1863 and again on 16 October 1867.[46] He died of heart disease on 3 February 1882 in Santa Rosa.[47] He is buried in Santa Rosa Rural Cemetery.[48]

8. Albert Perry Overton (served 1872–1875) was elected on 18 October 1871.[49] He was born in 1830 in Independence, Missouri, the son of Moses and Mary (Turner) Overton.[50] He died of heart disease on 13 April 1898 in Duncan Springs, Mendocino County, California and is buried in Santa Rosa Rural Cemetery.[51]

9. John Gotea Pressley (served 1876–1879) was elected on 20 October 1875.[52] He was born on 24 May 1833 in Williamsburg District, South Carolina, the son of John B. and Sarah (Gotea)

[43] "Official Vote of Sonoma and Mendocino Counties," *The Sonoma County Journal* (Petaluma, California), 18 September 1857, p. 2, cols. 4–5. Sonoma County, California, oath of office for William Churchman as County Judge, 30 March 1858; Sonoma County Archives, Santa Rosa.

[44] "Election Returns: Sonoma County – Official," *The Sonoma Democrat* (Santa Rosa, California), 6 October 1859, p. 4, cols. 1–2. Sonoma County, California, oath of office for William Churchman as County Judge, 3 October 1859; Sonoma County Archives, Santa Rosa.

[45] "Died," *The Sonoma Democrat* (Santa Rosa, California), 8 November 1873, p. 5, col. 2. The death notice reads: "CHURCHMAN – In Santa Rosa, Nov. 4, aged 55 years, 3 months and 6 days. Deceased was a native of Indiana, and came to California in 1853 and has been since the time of his death a resident of Sonoma County." Ancestry, *Find A Grave*, database with images (https://www.findagrave.com : accessed 22 November 2019), memorial 28601451, William Churchman (1820–1873), Santa Rosa Rural Cemetery, Santa Rosa, Sonoma County, California; gravestone photograph by Pamela Fowler Sweeney.

[46] "Sonoma County Election Returns," *The Sonoma County Democrat* (Santa Rosa, California), 31 October 1863, p. 2, col. 2. "Official Election Returns of Sonoma County," *The Sonoma Democrat* (Santa Rosa, California), 26 October 1867, p. 5, col. 2.

[47] "Death of C. W. Langdon," *The Sonoma Democrat* (Santa Rosa, California), 4 February 1882, p. 2, col. 4.

[48] The location of Judge Langdon's grave in Santa Rosa Rural Cemetery is unknown. His grave was noted as having been decorated on Memorial Day 1883. See, "Memorial Day," *The Sonoma Democrat* (Santa Rosa, California), 2 June 1883, p. 3, col. 2.

[49] "The Official Returns of Sonoma County," *The Sonoma Democrat* (Santa Rosa, California), 28 October 1871, p. 5, col. 3.

[50] *An Illustrated History of Sonoma County, California. Containing a History of the County of Sonoma from the Earliest Period of its Occupancy to the Present Time, together with Glimpses of its Prospective Future; with profuse Illustrations of its Beautiful Scenery, Full-Page Portraits of some of its most Eminent Men, and Biographical Mention of Many of its Pioneers and also of Prominent Citizens of To-day* (Chicago: The Lewis Publishing Company, 1889), 332 (hereinafter cited as *An Illustrated History of Sonoma County*).

[51] Sonoma County, California, Register of Deaths, No. 3, letter O, entry for Albert P. Overton, 13 April 1898; Sonoma County Archives, Santa Rosa. Ancestry, *Find A Grave*, database with images (https://www.findagrave.com : accessed 21 November 2019), memorial 66099413, Albert Perry "Boss" Overton (1830–1898), Santa Rosa Rural Cemetery, Santa Rosa, Sonoma County, California; gravestone photograph by Pamela Fowler Sweeney.

[52] "The Official Vote," *The Sonoma Democrat* (Santa Rosa, California), 30 October 1875, p. 5, col. 2.

Pressley.[53] He died of heart disease on 5 July 1895 while camping near Fort Ross, Sonoma County, California and is buried in Santa Rosa Rural Cemetery.[54]

---

[53] *An Illustrated History of Sonoma County*, 580.

[54] Sonoma County, California, Register of Deaths (1884–1902), letter P, entry for John Gotea Pressley, 5 July 1895; Sonoma County Archives, Santa Rosa. Ancestry, *Find A Grave*, database with images (https://www.findagrave.com : accessed 22 November 2019), memorial 16777037, LTC John Gotea Pressley (1833–1895), Santa Rosa Rural Cemetery, Santa Rosa, Sonoma County, California; gravestone photograph by G.Photographer.

Further Reading

Belknap, D. P. *California Probate Law and Practice. Being a Compilation of All the Statutes of this State, Relating to Probate Courts, the Organization and Jurisdiction Thereof, and Proceedings Therein, the Estates of Deceased Persons, Executors, Administrators, Guardians and Wills. With Notes of Judicial Decisions, and an Appendix of Forms.* San Francisco: Sterett and Butler, 1858.

Black, Henry Campbell. *A Dictionary of Law Containing Definitions of the Terms and Phrases of American and English Jurisprudence, Ancient and Modern.* 1st edition. St. Paul, Minnesota: West Publishing Co., 1891.

Blume, William Wirt. "California Courts in Historical Perspective." *Hastings Law Journal* 22 (No. 1, November 1970): 121–195.

Coy, Owen C. *Guide to the County Archives of California.* Sacramento, California: California Historical Survey Commission, 1919.

Davis, W. N., Jr. "Research Uses of County Court Records, 1850–1879, and Incidental Intimate Glimpses of California Life and Society, parts I and II." *California Historical Quarterly* 52 (No. 3, Fall 1973): 241–266 and (No. 4, Winter 1973): 338–365.

Rose, Christine. *Courthouse Research for Family Historians: Your Guide to Genealogical Treasures.* San Jose, California: CR Publications, 2004.

Sonoma County Genealogical Society. *Bonds of Guardianship.* Santa Rosa, California: Sonoma County Genealogical Society, no date.

Sonoma County Genealogical Society. *Index and Abstracts of Wills, Sonoma County, California, 1850–1900.* Westminster, Maryland: Heritage Books, Inc., 2007.

Sonoma County Genealogical Society. *Probate Records, Sonoma County, California, Index for 1847 to 1959, Volume 1: A–K.* Berwyn Heights, Maryland: Heritage Books, Inc., 2014.

Sonoma County Genealogical Society. *Probate Records, Sonoma County, California, Index for 1847 to 1959, Volume 2: L–Z.* Berwyn Heights, Maryland: Heritage Books, Inc., 2014.

Acknowledgments

The author thanks the staff of the Sonoma County History and Genealogy Library for access to the original Sonoma County Probate Court records utilized in the production of this publication.

About the Author

Steven M. Lovejoy is a retired chemist living in Sebastopol, Sonoma County, California. He is currently (2020) the president of the Sonoma County Genealogical Society and a Sonoma County Historical Records Commissioner. He holds a PhD in synthetic organic chemistry from the University of Washington and a Certificate in Genealogical Research from Boston University. He can be contacted at stevelov@comcast.net.

Index to the Probate Court Records of Sonoma County

Name	File #	Type	Fee Book & Register	Minute Book
Abbay, William C.	170	D	B: 121-122, 205-206, 305-306	E: 179, 182-183, 188, 191, 254, 279, 286, 337, 359, 409, 410, 414, 443, 446, 492, 505, 506-508
Abelbeck, F. D.	594	D	C: 426-427	I: 481, 501-502, 504, 550
Ackerman, B. Henry	460	D	C: 116-117, 252-253	H: 144, 173, 181, 186-187, 192, 193, 347-348, 360, 367, 427-430, 498, 499-501, 529-530, 546, 562, 563, 589-593
Ackerman, Harriet/Hattie Bell	884	M	D: 124	M: 144-145; N: 452-453, 482-483, 505, 511, 544; O: 143, 187-188, 222, 237-239
Ackerman, Lewis/Louis Dan	494	M	C: 186-187	F: 541; H: 367, 409-410; N: 197, 198, 254-256; O: 299-300
Ackerman, Mary Edith	884	M	D: 124	M: 144-145; O: 143
Ackerman, N. R.	754	D	C: 776-777	K: 244, 260-261, 263, 264, 381-382, 396-397, 404, 435; L: 30-31, 181-182, 585, 623; M: 5, 107, 204-206
Ackerman, Rebecca Jane	884	M	D: 124	M: 144-145; N: 452-453, 482-483, 505, 511, 544; O: 143, 187-188, 222, 237-239
Ackermann, Mary	288	D	B: 581-582	F: 531, 541, 543, 564, 570-571
Acton, Martha	697	D	C: 652-653	J: 499, 518-519, 523, 543-544
Adams, Samuel	343	D	B: 715-716	G: 66, 71, 80, 82, 93, 344, 348, 368
Adamson, Mary E.	186	M	B: 213-214	E: 313
Akers, Catherine (aka Findley, Katherine)	584	M	C: 404-405	I: 405-406, 475-476; O: 365, 382-383
Alexander, Cyrus	589	D	C: 414-415	I: 456-457, 484-486, 585; J: 191-192, 561, 570-572
Alley, Charles W.	336	M	B: 699-700; C: 212-213	G: 192; H: 264, 281, 282-284, 417, 443-445, 454, 484-485; J: 527, 535-536; K: 379; M: 468, 525; N: 553-554, 576; O: 277
Anderlini, Charles/Carlo	879	D	D: 118	M: 101-102, 142-143, 151, 167, 410, 411, 439-441, 572-573
Andres, Anton	966	D	D: 210	N: 483-484, 506, 512-513, 526, 539, 555-556, 571-572, 633-634
Archambeau, Peter T.	838	D	D: 76	L: 399, 417, 447, 552-553; M: 38, 631-632; N: 29, 55-57, 82-83; O: 305, 321, 341, 367, 377, 498-499, 512
Archer, Winston/Winson	369	D	B: 775-776	G: 198-199, 208; M: 227, 243-244

Name	File #	Type	Fee Book & Register	Minute Book
Armstrong, David	1015	D	D: 262	O: 233, 244, 293-294, 328, 332
Armstrong, Rosanna	578	M	C: 388-389	I: 375
Arnold, George W.	152	I	B: 49-50	E: 64, 82, 85, 100
Atherton, Albert W.	794	M	D: 30	L: 94-95, 103-104
Atherton, Dwight C.	794	M	D: 30	L: 94-95, 103-104
Aull, A. B.	432	D	C: 52-53, 214-215	G: 581, 583, 602, 623, 629; H: 63, 79, 80, 117, 149, 151-153, 489, 495-496, 513, 517-519
Aull, George E.	436	M	C: 60-61	G: 626, 629; H: 529, 597; I: 573-574, 582; J: 468; L: 471, 476-477, 508; O: 176, 193, 204
Aull, Laura	436	M	C: 60-61	G: 626, 629; H: 529, 597; I: 573-574, 582; J: 468
Aultenberger/Altenberger, Henry	765	D	D: 1	K: 313, 323-325, 331, 337-338, 441; L: 386-387, 400-401
Aynsley, John	910	D	D: 150	M: 561, 620; N: 63-64, 67, 68, 264, 376, 503-504, 509, 510, 549; O: 22, 55-58, 79-80
Bach, Frederick	674	D	C: 606-607	J: 392-393, 407, 413-414
Bacharino, Juan	440	D	C: 70-71	H: 31, 37, 162, 168-169, 210-211
Baillie/Bailee, George H.	146	D	A: 160; B: 15-16	E: 12, 19-20, 43, 491, 495-497
Baker, Isaac	205	D	B: 311-312, 381-382, 575, 797	E: 499, 518, 524; F: 15, 26-27, 56-57, 88, 89-90, 98, 99, 120, 151, 164, 168, 178-179, 292, 444, 453, 460-461, 534-535
Ballou, Volney James	902	D	D: 142	M: 282, 323-325, 395, 419; N: 366, 379-380, 391-393
Barnes, John J.	867	D	D: 107	L: 630-631; M: 3-5, 90, 106-107; N: 87-89, 109, 110-113
Barry, Ellen/Nellie Agnes	641	M	C: 526-527	J: 161; K: 332, 346, 391; L: 62-63, 75, 80-81, 93
Barry, Julia	641	M	C: 526-527	J: 161; K: 332, 346, 391; L: 62-63, 75, 80-81, 93
Barry, Mary Elizabeth	641	M	C: 526-527	J: 161; K: 332, 346, 391; L: 62-63, 75, 80-81, 93
Barry, Richard	521	D	C: 248-249	H: 560, 581-583, 586; I: 18-19, 69, 81, 278, 515, 526-527, 567, 586-587, 588; J: 181-185, 445

Name	File #	Type	Fee Book & Register	Minute Book
Barry, Susan Ann	641	M	C: 526-527	J: 161; K: 332, 346, 391; L: 62-63, 75, 80-81, 93
Barry, Thomas	641	M	C: 526-527; D: 40-41	J: 161; K: 332, 346, 391; L: 62-63, 75, 80-81, 95
Barry, William	641	M	C: 526-527; D: 40-41	J: 161; K: 332, 346, 391; L: 62-63, 75, 80-81, 92-93, 95
Bartlett, Caleb	1021	D	D: 268	O: 326-327, 344-345, 346, 449
Batchelder, Ezra D.	231	D	B: 407-408	F: 84, 103, 133, 138, 144-145, 280, 339, 346-348
Batchelder, Ira	229	D	B: 399-400	F: 68, 84
Bates, Laura	911	M	D: 151	M: 624-625; N: 27
Bates, Lydia Jane	483	D	C: 164-165	H: 293, 298, 349; I: 219-220, 250, 282, 292-295
Bates, Neely/Neeley	911	M	D: 151	M: 624-625; N: 27
Bates, Samuel H.	993	D	D: 238	O: 75, 94-95, 209-210, 386-387
Baylis, Theodore H.	608	M	C: 456-457	I: 561-562; J: 325
Baylis, Thomas F.	364	D	B: 765-766; C: 400-401	G: 172, 182-183, 188, 321, 324-325, 350-351, 605, 606, 630, 651-652; I: 119-121, 400, 401, 416-420, 482, 494, 505, 530-533, 538-539, 546-547, 557, 560-561, 563-564
Baylis, Thomas F.	615	D	C: 470-471	J: 5, 21, 558-559, 590, 613-615; K: 38-40, 47-48
Beaver, Lurania (heirs of)	26	D	A: 27	
Bedwell/Bidwell, James	93	M	B: 81-82	E: 108-109
Bedwell/Bidwell, John	93	M	B: 81-82	E: 108-109
Bedwell/Bidwell, Nancy	93	M	B: 81-82	E: 108-109
Beeson, Isaac	885	D	D: 125	M: 128, 164, 165-167, 316-317; N: 408, 455-466, 525-526
Beeson, J. B.	732	D	C: 726-727	K: 111, 121-122, 123, 152, 266-267
Bell, Albert K.	132	M	A: 144	D: 283-284
Bell, Henry H.	132	M	A: 144	D: 283-284
Bell, John W.	132	M	A: 144	D: 283-284
Bell, Louisa F.	132	M	A: 144	D: 283-284
Benson, Henry	530	M	C: 270-271	H: 576, 588-589
Benson, Josiah	530	M	C: 270-271	H: 576, 588-589
Benson, Laura	530	M	C: 270-271	H: 576, 588-589
Benson, Louis E.	530	M	C: 270-271	H: 576, 588-589
Benson, Martha E.	530	M	C: 270-271	H: 576, 588-589
Benson, Nathaniel	530	M	C: 270-271	H: 576, 588-589

Name	File #	Type	Fee Book & Register	Minute Book
Benson, William	530	M	C: 270-271	H: 576, 588-589
Bergreen, John F.	165	D	B: 95-96, 155-156	E: 146, 147, 149, 161, 174, 181, 241, 245-246, 352, 362, 371-373
Bicknell, Anna	652	M	C: 550-551	J: 216-217, 251, 287-289, 356
Bicknell, Charles J.	183	D	B: 181-182, 351-352	E: 292, 295, 312, 314, 324, 580, 593-594, 597, 607, 619-620; F: 197; M: 419; N: 160-162
Bicknell, Charles J.	652	M	C: 550-551	J: 216-217, 251, 287-289, 356; M: 419, 537-540; N: 144, 160-162
Bicknell, Ida	652	M	C: 550-551	J: 216-217, 251, 287-289, 356, 363-366
Biers/Byers, James	292	D	B: 589-590	F: 559, 582, 584, 592, 777
Bills, Sherman	561	D	C: 350-351, 576-577	I: 203-205, 217, 233-235; J: 107, 178-179, 190, 220-221, 223, 224-225, 315, 316, 330-332, 383, 400-401, 405-406, 434-440, 474-476, 480, 523-524
Bischoff, Frederick	32	D	A: 33	C: 8-9; D: 23, 24, 227, 246-247
Black, Henry	610	D	C: 460-461	I: 572; J: 2-3, 14, 113, 385-386, 407-408, 409-410
Black, Joseph Lenoir	514	D	C: 234-235	H: 536, 546-547, 555, 566; I: 4-7, 62-63, 75-78, 422, 425, 432-434, 460-461, 506-510
Blakeley, Eugene	912	M	D: 152	M: 625-626; N: 27-28
Blakeley, Martin L.	912	M	D: 152	M: 625-626; N: 27-28
Blakeley, Unity	912	M	D: 152	M: 625-626; N: 27-28
Boak, Samuel A.	23	D	A: 24	B: 143-144, 156-157, 327, 355-356
Bocock, James	972	D	D: 216	N: 527-528, 529, 539-540, 543, 551; O: 5, 27, 38, 104-105, 357, 373-374
Boggs, Anthony B.	606	D	C: 452-453	I: 540, 577-578; J: 86, 125-129, 194-196, 481, 488-490
Boggs, Joseph O.	1001	D	D: 246	O: 117, 130-131
Bolio, Maria/Mary	27	D	A: 28	B: 57, 107-108, 117
Bond, Joshua L.	625	D	C: 494-495	J: 49-50, 90-91, 96
Bond, Rezuba	837	D	D: 75	L: 398, 417-419; M: 80, 131-132
Bosworth, Albert H.	1009	M	D: 255	O: 185, 199, 350
Bosworth, Climena D.	1009	M	D: 255	O: 185, 199, 350
Bosworth, Fannie L.	1009	M	D: 255	O: 185, 199, 350
Bosworth, James O.	975	D	D: 220	N: 548, 561, 562; O: 62, 182-183, 199-203, 348

Name	File #	Type	Fee Book & Register	Minute Book
Bosworth, James O., Jr.	1009	M	D: 255	O: 185, 199, 350
Bosworth, Lorinda W.	1009	M	D: 255	O: 185, 199, 350
Bosworth, Viola	1009	M	D: 255	O: 185, 199, 350
Bottrell, Elizabeth	537	D	C: 288-289	I: 66-67; J: 278, 306, 317
Bousse, Frederick	4	D	A: 4	
Bowles, John	8	D	A: 9	
Boyden, Calvin W.	29	D	A: 30	B: 104-105, 112, 113-114, 164, 327, 353-354
Bradbury, J. C.	232	D	B: 413-414, 527-528	F: 94-95, 103, 114, 123, 132, 155, 177, 186, 187-190, 353, 362, 397, 411, 445, 456-457, 493-494
Brain, Samuel	953	D	D: 197	N: 260, 307-309, 310
Bray, Horrel	875	D	D: 114	M: 59-60, 86, 99, 158; N: 382-383, 413-414; O: 219-220
Bray, Mary	502	D	C: 202-203	H: 423-424, 443, 488, 491, 497, 519-520
Briggs, C. A.	1030	D	D: 277	O: 385, 400, 430, 437
Briggs, Edwin	991	D	D: 236	O: 39, 73, 83, 85, 97, 230-231, 254, 256, 267, 273-275
Bright, Samuel B.	384	D	B: 803-804	G: 251, 254, 266, 277-278, 438, 466-468, 515-516, 614, 642-643
Brink, Edward	347	D	B: 723-724, 727-728	G: 89, 112, 121, 334
Brokaw, Brogan J.	387	D	B: 809-810	G: 273, 282, 289, 308, 465, 469
Brooks, Henry C.	93	M	B: 35-36, 83-84	E: 108-109
Brooks, James	93	D	A: 106; B: 35-36, 97-98	D: 43, 57, 76, 93, 94, 199, 212-213, 254, 255, 270, 296-299; E: 70, 99, 108-109, 141-142, 262, 263, 289-290, 291
Brooks, Thomas J.	93	M	B: 35-36, 83-84	E: 108-109
Brown, Calvin H.	435	M	C: 58-59	G: 620, 622, 623, 631; H: 5-7, 29-30, 39-41
Brown, Daniel	780	M	D: 16	K: 420
Brown, James W.	780	M	D: 16	K: 420
Brown, Joseph H.	235	D	B: 431-432	F: 166, 167, 176, 180, 183, 191, 194-195, 446, 450, 468, 483, 522-523, 705, 719, 720
Brown, Martha E.	780	M	D: 16	K: 420

Name	File #	Type	Fee Book & Register	Minute Book
Brown, Mary R.	435	M	C: 58-59	G: 620, 622, 623, 631; H: 5-7, 29-30, 39-41
Brown, Oliver	435	M	C: 58-59	G: 620, 622, 623, 631; H: 5-7, 29-30, 39-41
Brown, Orrin	435	M	C: 58-59	G: 620, 622, 623, 631; H: 5-7, 29-30, 39-41
Brown, S. W.	208	D	B: 315-316	E: 511, 514-515, 530, 531, 536, 555
Brown, Samuel C.	239	D	B: 449-450	F: 219, 226-227
Brown, Thomas L.	435	M	C: 58-59	G: 620, 622, 623, 631; H: 5-7, 29-30, 39-41
Brown, Warren F.	567	D	C: 362-363	I: 249-250, 269-270, 272-273
Brumfield, Prisilla G. A.	706	M	C: 670-671	J: 572-573
Bruner, John	451	D	C: 96-97	H: 97, 116, 136, 142, 563, 595, 596; J: 318
Bruner/Brunner, Christian	33	D	A: 34	
Brunk, Hezekiah	520	D	C: 246-247	H: 557-558; I: 7, 29-30, 333, 374, 414-415; K: 226, 256, 261-262, 312-313, 341-342, 343-344, 363, 364-370
Brunner, Jacob	30	D	A: 31	B: 103, 107, 113, 125, 201, 213-214, 297, 316, 336, 363, 389
Brush, D. C.	1037	D	D: 284	O: 424-425, 437-438, 451
Bryant, Robert L.	1020	D	D: 267	O: 321-322, 329, 335-336, 461
Bugg, Buena Vista	206	M		
Bugg, Samuelar	206	M		
Bugg, Ulrica S. V.	206	M		
Burbank, Caleb	616	I	C: 472-473	J: 8, 497, 516, 522, 556, 565, 602; K: 225-226, 252-253, 293-294, 322-323, 442; L: 2
Burger, Abraham	298	D	B: 605-606; C: 218-219	F: 585, 597-598, 603, 616, 617, 625, 646, 784-785, 792-793; H: 373-374, 424-425, 459, 468-471, 480, 515-517, 532, 541-544
Burgess, Sebro G.	858	D	D: 97	L: 576-577, 618-620; M: 355, 422-423, 502-503, 550, 632-633; N: 239-240, 306-307, 332-334
Burk, Margaret	459	M	C: 114-115	H: 156, 183
Burnett, William	438	D	C: 66-67	H: 17, 26-27, 36, 85, 93-94, 127, 146-147, 160-161, 203, 248-249, 266

Name	File #	Type	Fee Book & Register	Minute Book
Burns, William K.	87	I	A: 99; B: 235-236, 383-384, 409-410, 411-412	B: 101, 102, 103, 108, 152, 162, 167, 171-172, 178, 245-247, 301-302, 307, 423, 427; C: 4; D: 25, 91; E: 542, 545-546, 571-572, 616, 622-623; F: 8, 32, 33, 74-76, 90, 92, 93, 95, 106-107, 116-117, 253, 301, 312-314
Burrus, James A.	461	M	C: 118-119	H: 174
Burrus, Mary C.	461	M	C: 118-119	H: 174
Burrus, William	28	D	A: 29	
Butler, James	801	D	D: 37	L: 85, 103, 296-297, 446-447; M: 290, 293, 322, 392-393
Butters, Thomas	31	D	A: 32	B: 143-144, 159, 165; D: 163, 189, 226, 231
Byrd, John	10	D	A: 11	
Byrns, James W.	843½	M	D: 82	N: 261-263
Caldwell, John G.	250	M	B: 481-482	F: 277, 278
Caldwell, Samuel T.	250	M	B: 483-484	F: 277, 278
Cameron, Alva O.	34	M	A: 34-37	B: 123
Cameron, David E.	34	M	A: 34-37	B: 123
Cameron, Mary E.	34	M	A: 34-37	B: 123
Cameron, Mary E. (now Fitch, Mary E.)	957	M	D: 201	M: 595, 620-621; N: 14, 40-41, 43-44, 45, 64-65, 84-85, 192-196, 203, 328-329
Cameron, Oliver P.	34	M	A: 34-37	B: 123
Cameron, Oliver P.	957	M	D: 201	M: 595, 620-621; N: 14, 40, 64-65, 85, 91, 196, 202, 204, 328
Cameron, Thomas P.	34	D	A: 34-37; B: 27-28	B: 58-59, 72, 79-80, 106, 119, 120, 121, 122, 123, 126-127, 128-129, 132-133, 134, 173; D: 79, 95, 112, 125, 156, 162, 171-174; E: 56, 66, 88-89
Cameron, William W.	34	M	A: 34-37	B: 123
Campbell, George Samuel	358	M	B: 751-752	G: 130
Campbell, Harry (alias Gamble, Hugh)	281	I	B: 567-568	F: 500, 583, 588
Campbell, Peter	237	D	B: 443-444, 513-514	F: 206, 215-216, 234, 238, 241, 262, 264, 270, 326, 343, 353, 362-363, 374, 448, 467-468, 499, 517-518, 567, 597, 599-600
Camron/Cameron, J. M.	951	D	D: 195	N: 242-243, 268-271, 339, 348-349; O: 234, 263-265

Name	File #	Type	Fee Book & Register	Minute Book
Cannon, Mary Ann	836	D	D: 74	L: 397, 462-463, 477-478; M: 51, 170, 179-181
Cantrell, P. H.	963	D	D: 207	N: 415, 454-455, 528, 619
Cantrell, Robert Jackson	893	D	D: 133	M: 224, 247-249
Carder, D. D.	946	D	D: 190	N: 198-199, 256-257, 264-265, 411-413, 543
Carney, Maurice	758	D	C: 784-785	K: 267, 292, 314, 339
Carriger, Solomon	25	I	A: 26	
Carrillo, Amelia C.	704	M	C: 666-667; D: 257	J: 557-558; K: 249, 274-275; M: 135, 177, 257-258, 359-360, 382-383, 524-525, 551, 552, 591; N: 22-23, 99-102, 154, 156, 171, 172, 175-178, 199-200; O: 51, 246, 266, 270, 273
Carrillo, Catherine A.	704	M	C: 666-667; D: 257	J: 557-558; K: 249, 274-275; M: 135, 177, 257-258, 359-360, 382-383, 524-525, 551, 552, 591; N: 156, 171, 172, 199-200; O: 51, 181, 193, 203-204, 218, 246, 266, 272, 273, 281, 319-320, 413, 441-443
Carrillo, Frank J./J. Frank	704	M	C: 666-667; D: 257	J: 557-558; K: 249, 274-275; M: 135, 177, 257-258, 382-383, 524-525, 551, 552, 591; O: 51
Carrillo, Frederick A.	704	M	C: 666-667; D: 257	J: 557-558; K: 249, 274-275; M: 135, 177, 257-258, 359-360, 382-383, 524-525, 551, 552, 591; N: 22-23, 99-102, 154, 156, 171, 172, 175-178, 199-200; O: 51, 246, 266, 271, 273, 460-461
Carrillo, Guadalupe	688	D	C: 634-635, 792-793	J: 469, 485, 513, 518, 528-529, 530-531, 532, 562; K: 241, 249, 273-274, 291-292, 310-311, 398-399, 408-410, 430, 443-445, 455-461; L: 208, 251, 266-268, 272; M: 258-264
Carrillo, Louisa A.	704	M	C: 666-667; D: 257	J: 557-558; K: 249, 274-275; M: 135, 177, 257-258, 359-360, 382-383, 524-525, 551, 552, 591; N: 22-23, 99-102, 154, 156, 171, 172, 175-178, 199-200; O: 51, 246, 266, 268, 273
Carrillo, Maria Ignacia Lopez	11	D	A: 12	

Name	File #	Type	Fee Book & Register	Minute Book
Carrillo, Mary F.	1008	D	D: 254	O: 186, 213-214, 244-245, 316, 317, 352-353, 412, 439-441, 474, 491, 500-502, 503
Carrillo, Mary F. (also Carrillo, Fannie B.)	704	M	C: 666-667; D: 257	J: 557-558; K: 249, 274-275; M: 135, 177, 257-258, 359-360, 382-383, 524-525, 551, 552, 591; N: 156, 171, 172, 199-200; O: 51, 246, 269, 273
Carroll, James	400	D	B: 835-836	G: 330-331, 343, 355; H: 281, 294-295, 314-319, 527
Carter, Andrew J.	1027	M	D: 274	O: 366-367, 393
Carter, Andrew Jackson	482	M	C: 162-163	H: 307, 319-320, 515; I: 119, 173, 240-241; K: 179, 208, 209, 244-246, 294; L: 416; M: 506-507
Carter, David	707	D	C: 672-673	J: 578, 590-591; K: 65, 165-166
Carter, Hansford/Handsford F.	193	D	B: 237-238, 287-288	E: 379, 398, 412, 413, 444, 446, 543, 553, 581, 602, 613; F: 2
Carter, Joseph	356	D	B: 747-748	G: 123, 207, 213-214, 223-224, 328, 341
Carter, Margaret L.	482	M	C: 162-163	H: 307, 319-320, 515; I: 119, 173, 240-241; K: 179, 208, 209, 244-246, 294-295; L: 416; M: 506-507
Carter, Mary E.	1023	D	D: 270	O: 333, 364, 394-395, 396, 397
Carter, Nancy V.	482	M	C: 162-163	H: 307, 319-320, 515; I: 119, 173, 240-241; K: 179, 208, 209, 244-246, 295; L: 416; M: 506-507
Carter, William F.	307	D	B: 627-628	F: 633, 639-640, 646, 652, 654, 791; G: 31, 44, 53, 63, 89-90
Case, Henry T.	19	D	A: 20	
Cash, Job	442	D	C: 74-75	H: 38, 44, 47
Cashdollar, Algia Beatrice	668	M	C: 588-589	J: 334
Casper, John	220	D	B: 365-366	E: 625; F: 9, 18-19, 41, 109, 182, 195, 196
Castens, Sophia	627	M	C: 498-499	J: 57, 80-81
Cathey, George	344	M	B: 719-720	G: 81, 96, 121
Cathey, James	344	M	B: 719-720	G: 81, 96, 121
Cathey, John	344	M	B: 719-720	G: 81, 96, 121
Cathey, Paralee	344	M	B: 719-720	G: 81, 96, 121
Cecil, John F.	133	D	A: 145; B: 77-78	D: 285, 300, 306, 322, 327, 331, 332; E: 117, 125, 127, 131, 150, 161-162, 172-173, 177

Name	File #	Type	Fee Book & Register	Minute Book
Christ, G. W.	276	D	B: 555-556	F: 461, 465, 469, 483, 495-496
Churchman, John	721	M	C: 704-705	K: 70-71
Churchman, Maggie	722	M	C: 706-707	K: 12-13, 47, 57-58
Churchman, William	659	D	C: 564-565	J: 250, 259, 308-309; K: 92-93, 123-127, 162-163, 164, 204-206; L: 188, 255, 256-261
Churchman, William	720	M	C: 702-703	K: 71
Clapper, Edward	153	D	B: 51-52	E: 66, 87-88, 105, 119, 150-151, 293, 303-304
Clark, Alice M.	1032	D	D: 279	O: 408-409, 430, 443, 462, 471, 515, 519
Clark, Andrew	522	D	C: 250-251	H: 559, 583, 584-585, 587
Clark, Charles P.	422	M	C: 32-33	G: 525, 529-530; H: 57, 175, 302, 336
Clark, Estella	735	M	C: 732-733	K: 121
Clark, Florence B.	422	M	C: 32-33	G: 525, 529-530; H: 57, 175, 302, 336
Clark, Frederick W.	735	M	C: 732-733	K: 121
Clark, Gertrude L.	735	M	C: 732-733	K: 121
Clark, James	643	D	C: 530-531	J: 166, 218-220, 313, 456, 457, 486
Clark, James M.	735	M	C: 732-733	K: 121
Clark, Margaret E.	735	M	C: 732-733	K: 121
Clark, Mary Alice	422	M	C: 32-33	G: 525, 529-530; H: 57, 175, 302, 336
Clark, Samuel G.	160	D	B: 73-74, 279-280, 321-322	E: 105, 116, 186, 423, 425, 433-434, 465, 467-468, 470-471, 482, 515, 534; F: 417, 420, 427, 441, 442-443, 454, 617, 632, 634, 689-690; G: 47, 462, 481-483; H: 175
Clark, William T.	37	D	A: 43; B: 211-212	B: 361-362, 365-366, 371, 388, 406-407, 415, 418; D: 34; F: 619, 625, 635, 648, 660
Clark, William T.	89	M	A: 101	D: 61
Clay, Jonathan	240	D	B: 453-454	F: 235, 256-257, 303, 354, 374, 401, 447, 457, 468, 476-477; K: 262
Clayton, Henry C.	154	D	B: 53-54	E: 83, 89, 107
Clover, Milton	842	D	D: 80	L: 456, 467-468, 470, 474, 478-479, 604; M: 267, 270-271, 336-341, 451, 516-519, 555, 577-578, 589-590, 629; N: 35-36, 67, 92-94

Name	File #	Type	Fee Book & Register	Minute Book
Clyman, Alice C.	457	M		H: 174, 309
Clyman, Frances M.	457	M		H: 174, 309
Clyman, James I.	457	M		H: 174, 309
Clyman, Mary	457	D	C: 108-109	H: 125, 149-150, 151
Cobb, Charles	683	D	C: 624-625	J: 446, 473-474, 612-613; K: 139-140, 169-170, 206-207
Cock, John	145	D	A: 159; B: 129-130	E: 7, 14, 18, 30, 31, 194, 214-215
Cocke, W. T.	1024	D	D: 271	O: 342, 356, 360
Cockerill, James A.	35	D	A: 38	B: 55, 56-57, 63, 95-96, 106, 110-111
Cockrill, Harrison	38	D	A: 44	B: 373-374, 378-379, 380-381; D: 338, 347, 355, 361, 364
Coe, Callie	685	D	C: 628-629	J: 461-462, 469
Coe, Frank H.	630	D	C: 504-505	J: 97-98, 130, 177-178, 247
Cofer, Elliott	218	D	B: 355-356	E: 610, 621, 631; F: 9, 19, 42
Cohen, Israel L.	1055	D	D: 302	O: 521
Cohen, Nettie	1054	M	D: 301	O: 520-521
Cohen, Rosa	1054	M	D: 301	O: 520-521
Colgan, Edward P.	592	D	C: 420-421	I: 474, 483-484, 487, 500-501
Collier, Ira	472	D	C: 142-143	H: 237, 260-261, 262, 287, 365; I: 70, 81, 93-95, 123-128
Collier, Shedrick F.	549	M	C: 318-319	I: 149-150; J: 622-624, 634; K: 27-30
Collins, Lafayette	338	D	B: 703-704	G: 39, 52
Colmar, Michael	669	D	C: 590-591	J: 342-343
Connelly/Connolly, Patrick	913	D	D: 153	M: 422
Conrad, Simon	609	D	C: 458-459	I: 566-567; J: 7-8, 12; N: 378-379, 408-410; O: 449-450
Cook, David P.	464	D	C: 124-125	H: 186, 202, 203
Cook, Ferriss Lee	125	M	A: 138	D: 228
Cook, George M.	687	D	C: 632-633	J: 466-467, 478-479, 483
Cook, James W.	125	M	A: 138	D: 228
Cook, Jesse G.	125	M	A: 138	D: 228
Cook, John H.	125	M	A: 138	D: 228
Cook, Lucinda E.	125	M	A: 138	D: 228
Cook, Mary Ann	125	M	A: 138	D: 228
Cook, Thomas A.	234	D	B: 421-422	F: 138, 145-146
Cook, William Y.	125	M	A: 138	D: 228

Name	File #	Type	Fee Book & Register	Minute Book
Cooke, Martin E.	39	D	A: 45-49; B: 25-26	B: 387-388, 390-391, 395, 396, 398, 423, 424, 428, 429; C: 2, 5-6; D: 130, 152, 155, 162, 163, 164-166, 167, 168, 190, 204, 215, 223-224, 255, 260-261, 262-263, 273, 308, 321, 325, 352-353, 362-363, 370, 371, 377-378; E: 29, 44, 101, 212, 317, 331-333, 441-442
Coon, Hugh	396	M	B: 827	G: 503
Cooper, James	36	D	A: 39-42; B: 45-46, 91-92, 127-128, 159-160, 341-342; C: 180-181	B: 313, 321, 322, 324, 326, 329-332, 347-348, 359-361, 400, 404-405, 426; C: 3-4; D: 65, 76, 82, 101, 120, 135, 155, 162, 168, 169, 175, 176, 179, 181, 185, 216, 219, 238, 248, 368; E: 63, 70-72, 90, 104, 107, 115, 120, 129, 136, 146, 147, 150-151, 152, 158, 169, 176, 181, 190, 193, 197, 208, 239-240, 244, 246, 252, 343-344, 376, 447; F: 648; G: 555, 589, 591, 597; H: 24, 28-29, 34, 41-42, 96, 274, 291, 296, 338, 380-384, 385-388, 391, 418, 493, 512; I: 72-73, 88-89, 109, 116, 117, 148, 173, 287-290
Cooper, John A.	491	D	C: 178-179	H: 349, 357
Cope, Harman C.	128	D	A: 140; B: 37-38	D: 264, 270, 284, 317; E: 58, 67, 92-93
Corban, Margaret Ann Kelly	316	M	B: 655-656	F: 712, 718
Corey/Cory, C. R.	999	D	D: 244	O: 113, 126, 135, 162-163, 243, 257-259, 341, 358, 362-363, 376-377
Cornelius, J. Clemens A.	308	D	B: 629-630	F: 636, 638, 640, 642, 700; G: 34
Coston, Addie	506	M	C: 210-211	H: 474
Coul, John B.	987	D	D: 232	O: 22-23, 63-64, 82-83
Covey, George	546	M	C: 310-311	I: 103; N: 6
Covey, Mary	546	M	C: 310-311	I: 103; N: 6
Cowles, Nathan C.	225	D	B: 391-392, 465-466	F: 62-63, 80, 82-83, 115, 120, 192-193, 233, 243, 354, 373-374, 392
Cox, George W.	710	M	C: 678-679	J: 603-604
Cox, Henry F.	147	M	A: 161	E: 29
Cox, John T.	171	D	B: 125-126, 167-168	E: 187, 191, 199, 203, 254, 271, 285
Cox, John W.	147	M	A: 161	E: 29

Name	File #	Type	Fee Book & Register	Minute Book
Cox, Richard	898	D	D: 138	M: 255, 280, 305, 347-348, 401-402
Crabtree, Mary Jane	148	M	A: 162; B: 451-452	E: 35; F: 228
Crisp, John B.	252	M	B: 487-488	F: 295, 315, 363, 394, 407-408; M: 585, 586; N: 46-47
Crisp, John W.	161	D	B: 75-76, 93-94, 379-380	E: 112-113, 124, 128, 140, 148, 197, 213, 316; F: 8, 17, 18, 41, 56, 73, 139, 142, 363; J: 339, 344, 354-355
Crisp, Maggie/Margaret E.	161	M	B: 515-516	F: 394, 407-408
Crisp, Sarah Judith	252	M	B: 501-502	F: 333, 345, 363, 394, 407-408
Crisp, William H.	175	M	B: 149-150	E: 220, 328; F: 363, 394, 407-408; M: 585, 593-594; N: 47-50
Crist, Rosa A.	872	I	D: 113	M: 48, 56-57
Crockett, Jeremiah T.	167	D	B: 113-114, 245-246	E: 168, 185, 381, 396-398
Crooks/Crook, J. J.	174	I	B:139-140	E: 216, 223-224, 241, 448, 450; F: 317-320
Csomortanyi, Louis	418	D	C: 24-25	G: 498, 503, 505-506, 547, 569-572, 610-612, 653; H: 4
Culligan, James	563	D	C: 354-355	I: 218-219, 263, 264-265
Cummings, William	562	D	C: 352-353	I: 210, 214-215, 217-218, 232, 248, 251, 266-267; J: 29-30, 38-41
Cunningham, Robert	421	D	C: 30-31	G: 517, 536, 537; H: 111, 135
Cutter, Joseph Smith	510	D	C: 226-227	H: 506, 525-526, 532; I: 421, 440; J: 187-188, 222-223, 470-471, 593; K: 3-4, 65-66, 395-396, 405-406, 437-438
Dagget/Daggett, Margaret	511	I	C: 228-229	H: 514, 520, 535; I: 109, 121, 122-123
Dagget/Daggett, Margaret	542	D	C: 300-301	I: 73, 101, 123, 180, 446; J: 213, 246, 255-256; L: 20-21
Daniels, Seneca	820	D	D: 58, 93	L: 216, 244-246, 528, 529, 581, 611, 633; M: 43, 110-111, 138-139, 254, 303, 334, 395, 555-559, 621; N: 14-15, 19-22, 600, 615-616
Davis, Edwin	677	M	C: 612-613	J: 411
Davis, Ella	677	M	C: 612-613	J: 411
Davis, Henry	677	M	C: 612-613	J: 411

Name	File #	Type	Fee Book & Register	Minute Book
Davis, James S.	804	D	D: 42	L: 133, 148-149, 212, 223-224, 294-295, 361-362, 479-480, 491, 521-523; M: 74
Davis, William K.	603	D	C: 446-447, 482-483	I: 526, 553-554, 563, 564, 575-576; J: 6, 10-11, 21, 26, 28, 34, 46-47, 48, 52, 60-63, 129, 131-132, 165-166, 406, 414-416, 424, 434, 462-463, 487-488
Davisson, Jesse	40	D	A: 50	B: 149, 153, 163, 179, 224, 260-261, 299-301, 356, 367-368
Day, Elias	658	D	C: 562-563	J: 249, 291-293, 324-325, 587, 597-599
Decker, James	215	D	B: 339-340	E: 558, 578-579, 616, 624; I: 159, 160, 175-177; J: 212
Defrees/Defries, Elizabeth	266	D	B: 533-534	F: 424, 452, 461, 521, 645, 659-660, 701, 706-708
Dellingham/Dillingham, John J. Lee	107	M	A: 123	D: 113; G: 234
Dellingham/Dillingham, John R.	107	D	A: 123	D: 113, 122, 291, 305, 312
Dellingham/Dillingham, Mary Elizabeth	107	M	A: 123	D: 113; G: 234
Dellingham/Dillingham, Sarah Emeline	107	M	A: 123	D: 113; G: 234
Dellingham/Dillingham, Susan Matilda	107	M	A: 123	D: 113; G: 234
Dellingham/Dillingham, William K.	107	M	A: 123	D: 113; G: 234
Delzell/Delzelle, Isaac A.	247	D	B: 471-472, 631-632	F: 251, 266, 409, 412, 419, 421, 436, 452, 477-478, 507, 553, 644, 657-658; G: 133, 137, 138, 160, 225, 235, 255, 266-267, 353-354, 391, 404, 413-414, 427, 441-443, 498, 520-522, 546
Dias, A. H. L.	907	D	D: 147	N: 81, 132, 133
Dickson, Charles H.	155	M	B: 55-56	E: 84, 112, 129
Dickson, Margaret	155	M	B: 55-56	E: 84, 112, 129
Dickson, Richard	151	D	B: 33-34, 103-104	E: 49, 65, 83, 91, 128, 150-151, 152, 202, 225-227, 255-256, 325, 334-336
Diederich/Diederick, John	667	D	C: 586-587	J: 326, 343-344, 346-347, 366, 568-569, 576-577; K: 72, 81-82, 241
Dodge, Simon B.	317	D	B: 659-660	F: 739, 743, 749-750; G: 105, 125
Dodge, William H. H.	467	D	C: 130-131	H: 218, 228, 230, 239, 269, 286-287, 312, 326-328, 375, 393-394
Dodge, William R.	449	D	C: 92-93	H: 89

Name	File #	Type	Fee Book & Register	Minute Book
Dollinger, Xavier	409	D	C: 4-5	G: 412, 427, 429, 434, 439-440, 461-462, 627, 633; H: 23, 73-76, 91-92
Domigan, Isabel	351	M		F: 453
Domigan, Rosa	351	M	B: 737-738	G: 105
Donaldson, John	749	D	C: 764-765	K: 221-222, 239-240, 308; L: 230, 261-263
Donner, George	673	D	C: 598-599	J: 358, 383-385, 405, 416, 618-619
Dopkins, Samuel	157	D		
Dovey, Stephen	448	D	C: 90-91	H: 85, 88, 97, 105-106, 119, 123, 124-125, 172, 185-186, 433-434, 459, 461-464, 565
Downing, John C.	784	D	D: 20	K: 446; L: 4-5, 9, 14, 33-34, 55, 137, 624; M: 36-37, 71, 97-99
Doyle, James	495	D	C: 188-189	H: 369, 378-379, 389; I: 166-167, 226, 298-303
Doyle, James	840	D	D: 78	L: 419, 443-444, 463, 479; M: 187-188, 202, 231-233, 326, 412, 630-631
Dozier, A. W.	716	D	C: 692-693	J: 625-626, 635-636, 637; K: 72, 76
Dozier, Roland	726	M	C: 714-715	K: 49, 56-57
Draper, Reuben	395	D	B: 827-828	G: 304, 320, 325
Dressel, Emil	419	D	C: 26-27	G: 494, 503-504, 507-508, 640; H: 263, 273, 299-300, 302-303, 328-332, 450
Drever, David	965	D	D: 209	N: 475, 514
Dumars, William	513	D	C: 232-233, 772-773	H: 537, 547-548, 550, 554; I: 406-407, 437, 439, 441-444, 559, 560, 579-582; J: 13, 30-31; K: 234-235, 276, 277-278
Dunn, John	691	D	C: 640-641	J: 484, 500-502
Dunne, John	870	D	D: 111	M: 19-20, 63-64, 71, 96-97, 103, 104, 411-412, 418, 433-434, 460, 521, 568-570
Dupont, John B.	498	D	C: 194-195	H: 418, 446-447
Durbin, Alexander	844	D	D: 83	L: 487, 502-503, 543, 613; M: 18-19, 48-50
Dyer, Claborn	1029	D	D: 276	O: 379, 408, 422-423, 436
Easley, Amanda M.	414	M	C: 18-19	G: 479; H: 55, 58
Easley, Sarah F.	414	M	C: 18-19	G: 479; H: 55, 58, 228-229
Easley, William P.	414	M	C: 18-19	G: 479; H: 55, 58, 228-229

Name	File #	Type	Fee Book & Register	Minute Book
Eddy, Decatur K.	101	D	A: 114; B: 67-68	D: 92, 103, 137, 152, 204, 272, 307, 320, 326; E: 100, 109, 111, 123, 132, 198, 224-225
Edmunson/Edmondson, Rufus C.	105	D	A: 121-122	D: 111, 123, 149, 160, 193, 268, 287, 327, 334, 341, 353-354; E: 11, 25
Edmunson/Edmonson, John C.	143	M	A: 157; B: 109-110	D: 343-344; E: 17, 161, 175-176
Edmunson/Edmonson, Richard P.	140	M	A: 154; B; 23-24	D: 344-345; E: 15, 16, 43, 52, 316; F: 798-800
Edmunson/Edmonson, Thomas Jefferson	141	M	A: 155; B: 141-142	D: 344; E: 16, 194, 205, 369, 386
Edmunson/Edmonson/Edmundson, Emily/Emma	142	M	A: 156; B: 131-132, 303-304, 429-430	D: 345; E: 17, 194, 206, 369, 387, 471, 479, 486, 487, 489, 491, 527, 541; F: 123, 126, 129, 146-147, 274-275, 278, 287, 294, 299, 370-371, 384; N: 73, 155, 163
Edmunson/Edmonson/Edmundson, Hugh R.	142	M	A: 156; B: 131-132, 303-304, 429-430	D: 345; E: 17, 194, 206, 369, 387, 471, 479, 486, 487, 489, 491, 527, 541; F: 123, 126, 129, 146-147, 274-275, 278, 287, 294, 299, 370-371, 384; N: 73, 155, 163
Edmunson/Edmonson/Edmundson, William F.	142	M	A: 156; B: 143-144, 479-480	D: 345; E: 17, 194, 205, 370, 385-386, 557, 599, 606, 626; F: 5, 6-7, 274-275, 279, 287, 294, 300, 368-370, 384; N: 72, 155, 162
Edwards, George	544	M	C: 306-307	I: 100, 113, 148-149
Edwards, Joseph	544	M	C: 306-307	I: 100, 113, 148-149
Edwards, Mary	544	M	C: 306-307	I: 100, 113, 148-149
Edwards, Thomas	559	D	C: 346-347	I: 170, 199, 207-208, 210; L: 411, 488-489, 503, 511-512, 513; M: 380-381, 396, 413, 424-426, 619-620; N: 17-18, 61-62, 123-124, 236, 274, 320-324, 399-401

Name	File #	Type	Fee Book & Register	Minute Book
Edwards, Uriah	398	D	B: 831-832; C: 324-325, 428-429	G: 328, 338, 342, 347, 504; H: 158, 176, 187, 191, 238, 258, 285, 301, 311, 355, 359; I: 117, 161-162, 199-200, 272, 279-280, 291, 321-322, 366-367, 375-376, 378, 388, 401-402, 447, 486-487, 535, 571-572; J: 329-330, 346, 353, 369, 391, 406, 426, 449-451, 589-590, 630; K: 147, 148-150
Edwards, Uriah, Jr.	545	D	C: 308-309	I: 100, 112-113, 367, 376-377, 378, 535-536
Elder, Charles G.	755	M	C: 778-779	K: 256-258
Elder, Helena M.	755	M	C: 778-779	K: 256-258
Elder, Jessie M.	755	M	C: 778-779	K: 256-258
Elder, John M.	755	M	C: 778-779	K: 256-258
Elder, Madison L.	755	M	C: 778-779	K: 256-258
Elder, Monroe C.	755	M	C: 778-779	K: 256-258
Elmore, Samuel O.	602	D	C: 444-445	I: 512, 533-535, 542-543, 549; J: 57-58, 206, 218, 225, 234, 244-245, 314, 326, 378-379
Engler, Mathias	1014	D	D: 261	O: 236-237, 259-260, 276, 277, 293, 297, 355
Epperley, Levi Oliver	864	M	D: 104	L: 624
Espy/Espey, John	301	D	B: 611-612; C: 684-685	F: 615, 622-623, 631, 633, 646, 721, 781, 791-792; J: 607-608, 624, 632-633; K: 356-357
Estes, C. F.	210	D	B: 319-320	E: 512, 523, 535; F: 59, 78, 111-113
Evans, Charles William	811	M	D: 49	L: 145-146, 156-158, 220, 238-241, 302, 314-316
Evans, David	178	D	B: 163-164, 277-278	E: 249, 267, 328, 411, 431
Evans, John Wirt	811	M	D: 49	L: 145-146, 156-158, 220, 238-241, 302, 314-316
Evans, Lucy Jane	811	M	D: 49	L: 145-146, 156-158, 220, 238-241, 302, 314-316
Evans, Thomas	782	D	D: 18	K: 423; L: 1, 9-10, 12, 104-107
Ewing, Ida B.	1052	M	D: 299	O: 510-511, 513-514
Face, Solomon	681	D	C: 620-621	J: 418-419, 457-459, 461, 465-466, 586, 626-627; K: 18-22

Name	File #	Type	Fee Book & Register	Minute Book
Fader, Anna H.	651	M	C: 546-547, 548	J: 190-191; K: 112, 143, 171-174; L: 482-483, 502, 536-537, 593-594; N: 253
Fader, Helen M.	651	M	C: 546-547, 548	J: 190-191; K: 112, 143, 171-174; L: 482-483, 502, 536-537, 593-594, 611, 612; M: 137, 197, 206-207, 254, 322-323, 348, 349-350; N: 192, 204, 207, 220, 253
Fader, Katie/Kate A.	651	M	C: 546-547, 548	K: 112, 143, 171-174; L: 482-483, 502, 536-537, 593-594, 611, 612; M: 137, 197, 206-207, 254, 322-323, 348, 349-350; N: 192, 204, 207, 220, 253
Fader, Victor V.	651	M	C: 546-547, 548	J: 190-191; K: 112, 143, 171-174; L: 482-483, 502, 536-537, 593-594, 611, 612; M: 137, 197, 206-207, 254, 322-323, 348, 349-350; N: 192, 204, 207, 220, 253
Fairbairn, Sarah M. E.	294	D	B: 595-596	F: 568, 579, 580, 717, 727-728
Falvey, Margaret	797	D	D: 33	L: 44-45, 74, 115-116, 300; M: 350-351, 377-378, 415-417, 565
Farquhar, Nora	444	M	C: 78-79	H: 61, 64
Farquhar, Winnifred	444	M	C: 78-79	H: 61, 64
Farris, Allen C.	501	D	C: 200-201	H: 423, 438, 439; I: 238; J: 344-345, 388-389, 416-417, 432, 440-442
Fawcett, Thomas	653	D	C: 552-553	J: 234, 257-258, 285, 306; K: 24
Fay, Bridget T.	588	D	C: 412-413	I: 438, 452-453
Fay, William Joseph	471	D	C: 140-141	H: 236, 260, 506; I: 66, 96-97, 168, 187, 189-191, 354-355
Feese, Joseph	693	D	C: 644-645	J: 485-486, 497, 498-499, 521
Ferguson, Peter	534	D	C: 280-281	I: 15-16, 40-41, 61-62, 538, 555-556, 584; J: 1-2, 36-37
Field, Effa	908	M	D: 148	M: 467, 510-511
Field, Erma	908	M	D: 148	M: 467, 510-511
Field, James	881	D	D: 120	M: 351-352, 400, 413, 427, 466-467, 513-514, 547, 550; N: 25-26, 105, 130-131, 166-169, 248-249, 270, 330-331, 360-365, 379, 418-421, 441-443, 517
Field, Thomas A.	713	D	C: 686-687	J: 619-620, 634; K: 34-36, 94; L: 51-52, 74, 79, 80; M: 50, 80-86, 315-316

Name	File #	Type	Fee Book & Register	Minute Book
Fike, Stephen Spencer	535	M	C: 282-283	I: 16, 32, 266; K: 83-84
Findley, David	584	M	C: 404-405	I: 405-406, 475-476; O: 365, 382-383
Findley, Elizabeth (aka Lashley, Elizabeth)	584	M	C: 404-405	I: 405-406, 475-476; O: 365, 382-383
Findley, Harvey	584	M	C: 404-405	I: 405-406, 475-476; O: 365, 384-385
Findley, Katharine (aka Akers, Catherine)	584	M	C: 404-405	I: 405-406, 475-476; O: 365, 382-383
Findley, Samuel	584	M	C: 404-405	I: 405-406, 475-476; O: 365, 384-385
Fine, Abraham	327	M	B: 677-678	F: 758, 760, 761; G: 167, 172, 181, 186, 215
Fine, Emeline	327	M	B: 683-684	F: 759, 760, 761; G: 166, 172, 180, 186, 215
Fine, Emsley	327	M	B: 679-680	F: 758-759, 760, 761; G: 166, 172, 180, 186, 215
Fine, John F.	217	D	B: 353-354, 419-420	E: 599, 606, 614; F: 13, 23, 24-25, 200, 215, 671, 677-678, 693, 726, 753-756, 772
Fine, Quin M.	2	D	A: 2	
Fine, William Petis	327	M	B: 681-682	F: 759-760, 761; G: 166-167, 172, 180-181, 186, 215
Fiscus, George W.	906	M	D: 146	M: 521-522
Fisher, Edward	267	D	B: 537-538	F: 430-431, 435, 453; G: 454, 462-464; H: 92-93; I: 506, 536-537
Fisk, Andrew Jackson	711	D	C: 680-681	J: 606-607, 608-609, 615-616, 625; K: 24-25; L: 67-68, 81, 94, 539-541, 556-558; M: 150-151
Fisk, Frank	711	M	C: 680-681	L: 558
Fitch, Anna	41	M	A: 51-52	B: 189-190, 191, 196-199, 220-221, 235-238, 256, 257-258, 268-276, 287, 288, 289, 290, 307-308, 320, 328-329, 341, 364, 389-390, 404, 409, 414-415; D: 357
Fitch, Charles	41	M	A: 51-52	B: 189-190, 191, 196-199, 220-221, 235-238, 256, 257-258, 268-276, 287, 288, 289, 290, 307-308, 320, 328-329, 341, 364, 389-390, 404, 409, 414-415; D: 357

Name	File #	Type	Fee Book & Register	Minute Book
Fitch, Clara	961	D	D: 205	N: 402-403, 432-433, 483, 489, 502-503, 508-509, 548, 565-566, 607-608; O: 21, 58-62, 80
Fitch, Clara	986	M	D: 231	O: 23-24, 64-65
Fitch, Henry D.	41	D	A: 51-52	B: 189-190, 191, 196-199, 220-221, 235-238, 256, 257-258, 268-276
Fitch, Herman	986	M	D: 231	O: 23-24, 64-65
Fitch, Isabel	41	M	A: 51-52	B: 189-190, 191, 196-199, 220-221, 235-238, 256, 257-258, 268-276, 287, 288, 289, 290, 307-308, 320, 328-329, 341, 364, 389-390, 404, 409, 414-415
Fitch, John B.	41	M	A: 51-52	B: 189-190, 191, 196-199, 220-221, 235-238, 256, 257-258, 268-276, 287, 288, 289, 290, 307-308, 320, 328-329, 341, 364, 389-390, 404, 409, 414-415; D: 357
Fitch, Joseph	41	M	A: 51-52	B: 189-190, 191, 196-199, 220-221, 235-238, 256, 257-258, 268-276, 287, 288, 289, 290, 307-308, 320, 328-329, 341, 364, 389-390, 404, 409, 414-415
Fitch, Josephine	41	M	A: 51-52	B: 189-190, 191, 196-199, 220-221, 235-238, 256, 257-258, 268-276, 287, 288, 289, 290, 307-308, 320, 328-329, 341, 364, 389-390, 404, 409, 414-415
Fitch, Mary E. (formerly Cameron, Mary E.)	957	M	D: 201	M: 595, 620-621; N: 14, 40-41, 43-44, 45, 64-65, 84-85, 192-196, 203, 328-329
Fitch, Natalia	986	M	D: 231	O: 23-24, 64-65
Fitch, William C.	986	M	D: 231	O: 23-24, 64-65
Fitzgerald, Edward	474	D	C: 146-147	H: 249, 270, 325-326, 511, 514; I: 399-400; J: 22-26, 115-116, 135-137
Flanery, Philip	478	D	C: 156-157	H: 289
Fleeman, William	173	D	B: 135-136	E: 196, 207; G: 134, 145, 158, 160, 184, 209, 210

Name	File #	Type	Fee Book & Register	Minute Book
Flege, Henry	348	I	B: 729-730; C: 62-63, 332-333	G: 96, 107, 345, 349-350, 547, 556, 557, 560-561, 564, 565, 573, 594-596, 614, 630, 646, 652, 654; H: 17, 18, 19-21, 157, 172-173, 205, 229, 237, 240, 250; I: 201, 218, 235-237; J: 609; L: 361, 387, 403, 437
Flege, Henry	712	I	C: 682-683	J: 627-629; K: 424-425
Flege, Mary Ann	712	I	C: 682-683	J: 627-629; K: 424-425
Flogdell, David Wickham	43	D	A: 55	B: 238-239, 249, 250, 317, 335, 382-383, 392-393, 395, 398-399
Flood, Joseph	745	D	C: 752-753	K: 177, 207-208, 213, 214; L: 127-129, 146-147
Flynn, James	406	M		I: 34-37, 262-263
Flynn, John	406	M		I: 34-37, 262-263
Flynn, Patrick	406	I	B: 847-848	G: 374, 387, 432, 464, 472-473; I: 13, 34-37, 262-263, 367-368; K: 411, 420-421
Forte, James	254	D	B: 493-494	F: 307, 325, 331, 332, 521, 545, 552, 559-560
Fowler, Edgar J.	675	M	C: 608-609	J: 399; K: 226-227, 246, 278, 279-280; L: 308-309, 353-354, 355-356; M: 354-355, 361; N: 477, 485, 505, 507-508; O: 227, 241, 358-359
Fowler, Phebe E.	686	D	C: 630-631	J: 466, 554, 639; K: 167; L: 214-215
Fowler, Richard	42	D	A: 53-54	B: 204, 211, 212, 240-241, 250, 276, 346-347, 363, 374, 377, 380, 381; D: 328, 329, 336, 347, 356, 363, 367, 369, 374; E: 6, 8
Fowler, Stephen L.	375	D	B: 787-788	G: 221, 226-227; J: 398, 486, 529, 533, 547, 552-554; K: 167, 175, 192-199, 276
Fowler, William Warren	675	M	C: 608-609	J: 399; K: 226-227, 246, 278, 279-280; L: 308-309, 354, 355-356; M: 354-355, 360; N: 477, 485, 505, 507-508; O: 227, 241, 358-359
Frankish, Robert	248	D	B: 473-474	F: 263, 265, 281-282
Frasier, Addie E.	601	M	C: 442-443	I: 511-512, 519-521, 530
Frasier, Julia A.	590	D	C: 416-417	I: 459-460, 479-480, 481; J: 361
Frasier, William J.	601	M	C: 442-443	I: 511-512, 519-521, 530

Name	File #	Type	Fee Book & Register	Minute Book
Freeland, Albert Clark	117	M	A: 133; B: 35-36	D: 197, 199, 236; E: 3, 8, 50-51
Freeland, Arnold Clark	44	D	A: 56	B: 401, 402-403, 417-418; D: 26, 41, 50, 70, 89, 127, 132, 145, 161, 191
Freeland, William	114	D	A: 130-131	D: 170, 180, 182, 196, 201, 202, 243, 256, 281, 285, 289-290, 303, 306, 368, 372-373
French, Ellen	670	D	C: 592-593	J: 349
Frost, Thomas	381	D	B: 797-798	G: 237, 248
Fruits, Jacob	817	D	D: 55	L: 210, 226-227, 251-252, 270-271, 280-281, 310, 316, 333-334, 491, 508, 514, 515-517, 519; M: 88, 108-110; O: 171
Fruits, John S.	376	M	B: 789-790	G: 220
Fruits, Robert Francis	376	M	B: 789-790	G: 220
Fullagar, Elizabeth	576	M	C: 384-385	I: 331; J: 426
Fuller, Thomas	775	D	D: 11	K: 381, 399, 401-402
Fulton, Richard	390	D	B: 817-818	G: 285, 292-293
Furber, George Campbell	701	D	C: 660-661	J: 530, 559, 563-564, 577-578
Galloway/Gallaway, Allen Rector	746	M	C: 754-755	K: 182-183
Galloway/Gallaway, Amanda Alice	746	M	C: 754-755	K: 182-183
Galloway/Gallaway, Andrew Jackson, Jr.	746	M	C: 754-755	K: 182-183
Galloway/Gallaway, Nancy Elizabeth	746	M	C: 754-755	K: 182-183
Gamble, Hugh (alias Campbell, Harry)	281	I	B: 567-568	F: 500, 583, 588
Gant, John	3	D	A: 3	
Garcia, Frederick	9	D	A: 10	
Gaskill/Gaskell, Abigail/Abigal	539	D	C: 294-295	I: 63, 85-87, 110-111, 281; J: 90, 110, 404
Gauldin Benjamin F.	179	M	B: 165-166	E: 251
Gauldin, John V.	179	M	B: 165-166	E: 251
Gauldin, Martha Ann	179	M	B: 165-166	E: 251
Gauldin, Willis Wilson	179	M	B: 165-166	E: 251
Gaulia, George	628	D	C: 500-501	J: 60, 93-95, 387-388, 547-548; O: 481-482
Gerl, Charles	769	D	D: 5	K: 333, 371-372, 373; L: 25
Gibson, George	158	D	B: 61-62, 191-192, 373-374	E: 89, 108, 112, 291, 299, 310, 327, 336-337, 370, 511, 520-521; F: 10, 20-22
Gilbert, Jacob	727	D	C: 716-717	K: 55-56, 92, 103-104, 109-110; M: 548, 597-598

Name	File #	Type	Fee Book & Register	Minute Book
Gilbert, Samuel W.	645	D	C: 534-535	J: 175, 199-200, 206, 214-215, 232, 247, 408-409
Gilham, J. B.	856	D	D: 95	L: 555, 589-590, 613-614, 616-617, 627-628; M: 66-67, 131, 296-298, 332-334, 484-485
Gill, Antonette	504	M	C: 206-207	H: 453, 471-472, 563; K: 108-109
Gill, George	447	D	C: 88-89	H: 86, 91, 100, 126, 147-148, 289, 304-305, 371, 395-396, 420-421, 445, 452-454, 464-468; I: 340-341
Gilleland/Gilliland, John M.	45	D	A: 57	B: 61-62, 175, 184, 315, 335, 342, 349, 357-358
Giovanari, Pietro	477	D	C: 154-155, 366-367	H: 274, 280-281, 296, 324, 325, 333-334, 339-340, 408, 510, 523-525, 544-545, 551-553; J: 262-263, 264, 306-307, 310-313; K: 158-159
Gird, Henry S.	166	I	B: 99-100, 151-152, 207-208	E: 154, 155, 160, 170, 201, 213, 220, 221, 235, 242, 251, 257, 262, 269, 270, 280, 286, 299, 349-351
Glasscock/Glascock, William	408	D	C: 2-3	G: 387, 390, 401, 402, 426, 430, 490-491, 608-609, 621, 637-639
Glover, A. B.	850	D	D: 89	L: 511, 529-530, 548; M: 51, 222-223; O: 276, 289-290
Glynn, Michael	994	D	D: 239	O: 85, 104, 109, 115, 374-375
Goddard, Albert D.	795	M	D: 31	L: 32-33
Goddard, Frank W.	795	M	D: 31	L: 32-33
Goddard, Jesse P.	795	M	D: 31	L: 32-33
Goddard, Wellman	795	M	D: 31	L: 32-33
Goddard, William B.	411	D	C: 10-11	G: 433, 440-441, 458-459, 484, 488-490, 535, 551, 560, 568-569; H: 17, 27-28, 159, 165, 176, 177-178
Godwin, Frederick Oscar	770½	M	D: 6	K: 357
Godwin, Henry Talmond	770½	M	D: 6	K: 357
Godwin, Hiram Ladd	770½	M	D: 6	K: 357
Golden, Thomas	982	D	D: 227	N: 622, 623, 630, 631; O: 52, 162, 181, 193, 217, 241, 457, 506-507, 512-513
Gormley, Martin F.	46	D	A: 58	B: 71-72, 82, 84, 106, 145, 181-182, 194-195, 293-294, 316, 409-410, 411-412, 423

Name	File #	Type	Fee Book & Register	Minute Book
Gossage, Zephaniah	851	D	D: 90	L: 527-528, 569-571; M: 42, 253, 426, 451, 480-482, 604-605
Graham, Ann	637	D	C: 518-519	J: 120-121, 140-142
Grant, Fergus	914	D	D: 154	N: 127-128, 152-153, 318-319, 344-346
Grant, Henry D. F.	296	M	B: 601-602	F: 577-578, 628, 722; G: 69-70, 83-86, 212-213; H: 490, 521-522
Gray, Anderson	162	D	B: 85-86, 189-190	E: 122, 137, 201, 217, 221, 337, 357-358
Gray, Hugh	306	D	B: 623-624, 839-840	F: 621, 623, 630, 650; G: 131, 145; H: 473, 474; I: 147-148; J: 242
Greathouse, George L.	1017	D	D: 264	O: 301, 314, 329, 334-335, 349, 360
Green, Alexander M.	462	D	C: 120-121, 330-331	H: 179, 185, 192, 205, 211, 216, 217, 350, 413-416, 435-437; I: 30-31, 79, 136, 137-141, 215-216, 276, 307-311, 478-479, 488, 489-493, 503
Green, Henry A.	48	D	A: 60-61	B: 65, 176, 186, 187, 189, 190-191, 199-200, 203, 212, 221-222, 235, 242, 248, 284, 291, 302-303
Gregory, Ann	761	D	C: 790-791	K: 286, 342, 346-347, 378, 392-393; L: 111, 125, 143-144, 152, 173, 177-178
Griffith, James A.	269	I	B: 541-542	F: 438-439, 444
Griffith, James A.	402	D	B: 839-840	G: 365, 370, 377, 392-394
Grissom, William	800	D	D: 36	L: 76, 89, 120, 122-124, 412-413, 428, 471, 502, 545, 572-574; M: 373-374
Gropp, Charles	829	I	D: 67	L: 228, 301, 376-377; M: 307, 342-344, 345, 497, 503-504, 585, 618; N: 1-4, 5, 80, 114-116, 126-127, 143-144, 147-149, 150
Grover, Benjamin Franklin	49	D	A: 61	B: 400-401, 402, 408, 409; D: 309, 333
Grover, James Madison	127	M	A: 139	D: 254
Grundy, Thomas E.	945	D	D: 189	N: 350, 373-375, 414-415, 444-446
Guinnett/Winnett/Winett, Nancy Ann	47	D	A: 59	B: 166, 174, 184-185, 251-252; D: 47, 48, 58
Haar, Martin	970	D	D: 214	N: 523, 535-537, 542-543, 578-579; O: 70-71, 375, 406-408, 521
Haight, M. H. (Dr.)	654	D	C: 554-555	J: 241-242

Name	File #	Type	Fee Book & Register	Minute Book
Hand, Samuel	53	D	A: 65	B: 222, 239-240, 283-284, 285-286, 291, 292, 303-304, 317, 325, 388, 393-394; C: 10-11, 33
Haraszthy, Frances	983	D	D: 228	N: 629; O: 6, 37, 72-73, 84
Hardcastle, Job N.	698	I	C: 654-655	J: 504-505, 526, 592; K: 1-2, 73-74
Hardin, George Milton	283	M	B: 571-572	F: 505, 528, 543; H: 44
Hardin, Henry	149	D	B: 13-14, 79-80, 81-82	E: 38, 52-53, 120, 280, 282-283, 284, 305-306; F: 671-672, 699, 709-711
Hardin, Stonewall Jackson	283	M	B: 571-572	F: 505, 528, 543
Hardin, William Jefferson, Jr.	256	D	B: 497-498	F: 329, 345-346, 497, 501, 505-506
Harmon, Martha	209	D	B: 317-318	E: 512, 516, 526
Harper, Reuben R.	102	D	A: 115-118	D: 96, 108, 126, 161, 170, 184, 202, 233, 235, 249, 280, 294-295, 313-314, 320, 341, 349, 354, 360, 370; E: 6, 9, 10, 12, 20, 25, 27, 28
Harris, Ephraim Drake	303	D	B: 615-616	F: 618, 624, 637, 642, 647, 669, 670, 746, 751
Harris, Thomas	52	D	A: 64	B: 59-61, 65, 106, 131, 167-168, 187, 205, 217-218
Harrison, Johanna	997	D	D: 242	O: 100, 120, 121, 151-152, 169, 393-394
Harvey, Alexander H.	554	D	C: 336-337	I: 182, 197-198, 210, 265, 317-321, 351-353; J: 11, 14-16
Harvey, Joel	644	D	C: 532-533	J: 167, 215, 221-222, 260, 580-581, 593-594, 610-612; K: 4-5
Harvey, Llewyllen/Lewellyn B.	916	D	D: 156	M: 610; N: 6-7, 65, 76-79, 124-125, 134, 142-143, 416-417, 446-451
Harvey/Hervey, Ella	748½	M	C: 762-763	K: 247-248, 259; L: 207-208, 271-272
Hasbrouck, Acelia	1033	D	D: 280	O: 404-405, 429-430
Hastings, Isaac	536	D	C: 286-287	I: 19-20, 84-85, 146-147, 304-305, 438, 453-454
Hatfield, Francis J.	596	M	C: 432-433	I: 499
Hatfield, Joseph A.	596	M	C: 432-433	I: 499
Hatfield, Rebecca	596	M	C: 432-433	I: 499
Hatfield, William P.	596	M	C: 432-433	I: 499
Hausch, Anna Bell	635	M	C: 514-515	J: 113-114
Hausch, Charles Henry Joseph	635	M	C: 514-515	J: 113-114
Hausch, Elsey	635	M	C: 514-515	J: 113-114
Hausch, Flora	635	M	C: 514-515	J: 113-114

Name	File #	Type	Fee Book & Register	Minute Book
Hausch, Hannah May	635	M	C: 514-515	J: 113-114
Hausch, Henrietta	635	M	C: 514-515	J: 113-114
Hawkins, Jesse	342	D	B: 713-714	G: 54, 64-65, 68-69, 71-72, 183-184, 217, 230, 240
Hays/Hayes, Samuel M.	481	D	C: 162-163	
Heald, Elizabeth	54	D	A: 66	B: 346, 348-349, 370; D: 116, 136
Heald, George William	196	M	B: 247-248, 371-372, 535-536; C: 312-313	E: 404, 406, 407, 416, 441, 630; F: 5, 30-31, 71, 87-88, 205, 213-214, 268-269, 320, 331, 341-342, 426, 635; G: 216, 403; H: 16, 301-302, 359-360, 399-401, 505-506; I: 2-3, 11-12, 44-47, 103-107, 573, 578-579; J: 137, 467-468; K: 317-318
Heald, Harmon G.	134	D	A: 146-147; B: 105-106, 243-244	D: 286, 310, 323-324, 355, 361; E: 12-13, 33, 34, 189, 209, 222, 317-320, 342, 363-364, 381, 400-403, 612-613
Heald, John Edson	599	M	C: 438-439	I: 504-505
Heffel, Robert	865	D	D: 105	L: 625; M: 21-23, 116-117, 311, 376, 403-407, 515-516
Hegeler, Gerhard	627	M	C: 498-499	J: 57, 80-81
Hegeler, John Henry Jacob	612	D	C: 464-465; D: 185	I: 582-583; J: 18-20, 225-226, 482; K: 284-285, 290-291, 297, 325, 355, 374-375; M: 117, 197, 224-225, 240, 280-281, 326, 356, 357-358; N: 84, 114, 229-230, 263, 299-304
Hegeler, Maria del Carmen	611	D	C: 462-463	I: 573; J: 17-18, 19; N: 588, 600, 618, 633; O: 48-49
Held, Henrietta Georgina	750	M	C: 766-767	K: 223, 232-233; O: 216, 221, 222, 260-261, 290
Hellsten, Charles	915	D	D: 155	M: 474, 485, 519-521; N: 103-104, 129, 169-171, 234, 404-405, 470-474, 485-487
Hembree, Andrew Thompson	657	D	C: 560-561	J: 248-249, 289-291
Hendley, John	736	D	C: 734-735	K: 129, 150, 159-161, 211, 255; N: 624, 634; O: 7, 380, 387-388, 406, 417-419
Hennessey, Daniel	325	D	B: 673-674, 813-814	F: 774, 778-779, 797-798, 802; G: 40, 61, 257-258, 275
Henry, James, Sr.	453	D	C: 100-101	H: 95, 99, 104, 136, 164

Name	File #	Type	Fee Book & Register	Minute Book
Herren, William G.	455	D	C: 104-105	H: 121, 129, 250-251, 252, 269-270; I: 33-34, 152-155, 156-158
Herron, Amy	790	M	D: 26	L: 3, 15-16, 84, 107-110, 154-155, 171-172
Herron, Belle	790	M	D: 26	L: 3, 15-16, 84, 107-110, 154-155, 171-172
Hershberger, Charles	947	M	D: 191	N: 188
Hershberger, Frank	947	M	D: 191	N: 188
Hesler, Philip	223	D	B: 385-386	F: 34, 36, 53, 58, 78, 209, 221-222
Hiett, George	541	D	C: 298-299	I: 71, 101-103, 576, 591-592; J: 367, 398-399, 401-403
Higara/Higgara, Nicholas	51	D	A: 63	B: 106, 108-109, 115-116
Hilby, Agatha M.	488	M	C: 174-175	H: 312, 338, 351-352, 355
Hilby, Francis M.	204	D	B: 301-302	E: 479, 486, 492, 493, 516-517; F: 12, 28-29
Hilby, Francis M.	488	M	C: 174-175	H: 312, 338, 351-352, 355
Hill, Amos	821	I	D: 59	L: 583, 610; M: 105, 149, 167, 475-476, 529-532
Hill, Anita	772	M	D: 8	K: 380
Hill, Joshua G.	1040	D	D: 287	O: 455-456, 470-471
Hinkston, Nancy	918	I	D: 158	N: 131, 137-138
Hinton, Otho	280	D	B: 565-566	F: 494, 498-499, 513, 649
Hoag, Hannah A.	1039	D	D: 286	O: 456, 473, 480-481, 512, 529-530
Holland, Hugh L.	781	D	D: 17	K: 421-422, 432, 433-434
Hollgreve, Henry	253	D	B: 489-490	F: 298, 326-327
Holliday, Joseph	360	D	B: 757-758; C: 578-579	G: 120, 135, 136, 250, 253, 363-364, 384-386; H: 279; J: 131, 158, 163, 164-165, 200, 204-205, 315-316, 336-337, 379-382, 585-586, 594-596; K: 176, 329-330, 342; L: 226, 251, 275-276
Hollister, Samuel E.	823	D	D: 61	L: 270, 285
Holloway, Archibald D.	99	D	A: 112-113; B: 47-48	D: 90, 102, 129, 139, 265, 270, 275, 288, 310, 316-317; E: 64, 79-81
Holloway, George W.	129	M	A: 141; B: 5-6	D: 265-266; E: 37, 40, 58, 60, 67
Holloway, Henrietta E.	129	M	A: 141; B: 5-6	D: 265-266; E: 40, 58, 60, 67
Holloway, Mary E.	129	M	A: 141; B: 5-6	D: 265-266; E: 37, 40, 58, 60, 67
Holman, Isaac A.	164	D	B: 89-90, 349-350	E: 130, 145, 148-149, 171, 525, 535, 548, 570, 576, 609

Name	File #	Type	Fee Book & Register	Minute Book
Holmes, Elizabeth	565	D	C: 358-359, 574-575	I: 235, 278-279, 324-325, 377, 386-387, 517-519, 529-530, 557; J: 9, 85, 96-97, 105-106, 123, 232, 299-305, 332-333, 419-424
Holser, Conrad	320	D	B: 665-666	F: 746, 756
Hood, Albert	843	M	D: 81	L: 464, 466, 523
Hood, Mary	843	M	D: 81	L: 464, 466, 523
Hood, Sarah	843	M	D: 81	L: 464, 466, 523
Hood, Stella Blanche	888	M	D: 128	M: 162-163
Hooper, Frances Mary	1007	D	D: 252	O: 177-178, 188-189, 295, 461-462, 478-480
Hooser, Joseph	212	D	B: 325-326	E: 524, 600, 607; F: 59, 79, 111, 128, 148, 163-164
Hooten, Jesse	385	D	B: 805-806	G: 243, 252-253, 494-495
Hopper, Climama/Climena	863	M	D: 103	M: 119-120, 140-142, 187, 295, 353, 378-380; N: 23-24, 62-63
Hopper, Edward	863	M	D: 103	M: 119-120, 140-142, 187, 295, 353, 378-380; N: 23-24, 62-63
Hopper, Emma Belle	863	M	D: 103	M: 119-120, 140-142, 187, 295, 353, 378-380; N: 23-24, 62-63
Hopper, Eugene	863	M	D: 103	M: 119-120, 140-142, 187, 295, 353, 378-380; N: 23-24, 62-63
Hopper, Thomas B.	863	D	D: 103	L: 617, 636-637; M: 14, 32, 58-59
Hotell, David	332	D	B: 693-694	G: 1, 11, 16, 28-29, 30, 37-38, 163-165, 179, 193-195, 196
Howel, Albia	431	M		K: 403, 407-408
Howell, Albinia E. L.	431	D	C: 50-51, 82-83	G: 566, 579-580, 588-589, 598, 599, 607; H: 139-141, 193, 307, 345-347, 502-503; K: 267-268, 301-306
Howell, L. V. H.	431	M		K: 403, 407-408
Howell, Mabel E.	431	M		K: 403, 407-408
Howell, Margaret L.	431	M		K: 403, 407-408
Howes, William F.	1048	D	D: 295	O: 506
Hrotis/Hortes, Nicolas/Nicholas	903	D	D: 143	M: 312, 331-332, 345-346, 505, 532, 618-619, 629-630; N: 65, 96-97
Hudson, Ann	538	D	C: 290-291	I: 62, 74-75; J: 350; K: 321, 400, 407, 415, 438-439, 440
Hudson, C. E.	847	D	D: 86	L: 500, 531-533; M: 198-199, 276, 369-373; N: 375, 383-389

Name	File #	Type	Fee Book & Register	Minute Book
Hudson, David A.	1013	D	D: 260	O: 212, 225, 228, 242, 386, 402-403
Hudson, Henry Walker	529	M	C: 266-267	H: 575, 594
Hudson, Martin	517	D	C: 240-241, 422-423	H: 549, 556, 568, 574, 597-598; I: 3-4, 42-43, 53, 98, 107-109, 181, 476-477; K: 72-73, 86-87, 88, 111, 116-117, 185-188; O: 160, 177, 190, 191-192, 217
Hudson, Mehatabel J. M.	964	M	D: 208	N: 432, 443
Hudson, Samuel	747	I	C: 758-759	K: 201
Hughes, John C.	50	D	A: 62	B: 72, 77-78, 85, 106, 109, 171, 176
Hughes, Josephine	489	M		F: 522
Humphries, William	291	D	B: 587-588	F: 556, 572, 574, 618, 663
Hunt, Charles	580	D	C: 392-393	K: 134-135, 145-146, 164-165
Hunt, Charles A.	580	M	C: 392-393	K: 170-171; L: 473, 492-493
Hunt, Charles William	564	M	C: 356-357	I: 237, 238
Hunt, Francis Willard	564	M	C: 356-357	I: 237, 238
Hunt, James B.	564	M	C: 356-357	I: 237, 238
Hunt, Lottie Elizabeth	564	M	C: 356-357	I: 237, 238
Hunt, Sarah Catherine	564	M	C: 356-357	I: 237, 238
Hunter, Elizabeth A.	525	D	C: 258-259, 760-761	H: 570, 583, 585-586, 587; I: 232-233, 588-589; J: 110-111, 123, 153-157, 390-391
Hunter, James	380	D	B: 795-796	G: 235, 248-249, 431, 434, 455, 464, 485
Hunter, Olin M.	525	M		I: 371; K: 212, 217
Hunter, Wilbur L.	525	M		I: 65-66, 370, 371; K: 212, 217-218
Hurd, Charlotte Psyche	738	M	C: 738-739	K: 134
Hurd, George Henry	738	M	C: 738-739	K: 134
Hurd, Isabella	702	D	C: 662-663	J: 532-533, 541-543; K: 59-60, 118, 131-134
Hurd, Lizzie Jane Taylor	738	M	C: 738-739	K: 134
Hurn, John F.	278	M	B: 561-562	F: 471, 491-492
Hurn, Seth R.	278	M	B: 561-562	F: 471, 491-492
Hurn, Sibbie E.	278	M	B: 561-562	F: 471, 491-492
Hurn, Solomon F.	278	M	B: 561-562	F: 471, 491-492
Hurn, William M.	278	M	B: 561-562	F: 471, 491-492
Hutchinson, A. F.	742	D	C: 746-747	K: 153-155; L: 303, 356-358
Hutton, Sarah L.	861	D	D: 101	L: 582, 605, 614-615
Ingoldsby, Charles	968	D	D: 212	N: 497-498, 513, 544

Name	File #	Type	Fee Book & Register	Minute Book
Ingram, J. S.	500	D	C: 198-199	H: 424, 437
Ingram, John	891	D	D: 131	M: 212, 245-246, 247, 352-353; N: 257-259
Irwin, Archibald Boyd	573	D	C: 376-377	I: 297-298
Isaacs, Louis	919	M	D: 159	M: 583-584, 599-600
Isaacs, Marks	919	M	D: 159	M: 583-584, 599-600
Jackson, Abraham Joseph	587	M	C: 410-411	I: 430, 435-436
Jackson, Charity	55	D	A: 67; B: 69-70	B: 352, 365, 373, 399, 414, 419; E: 101, 109, 110-111, 123, 133-136
Jackson, Fanny Victoria	587	M	C: 410-411	I: 430, 435-436
Jackson, Gideon	587	M	C: 410-411	I: 430, 435-436
Jackson, Lorenzo	340	D	B: 709-710, 713-714	G: 54, 64, 66, 230, 241
Jackson, Margaret	587	M	C: 410-411	I: 430, 435-436
Jackson, Mary Jane	587	M	C: 410-411	I: 430, 435-436
Jackson, Robert	585	D	C: 406-407	I: 420, 429-430, 435; J: 95, 102, 107-108, 243-244, 255, 274-277, 412-413
Jackson, William	379	D	B: 793-794	G: 224-225; H: 77, 83
James, Charles A.	793	D	D: 29	L: 26-27, 70-71, 107, 116, 327-328, 360-361
Jarvis/Jarvais, William	393	I	B: 821-822	G: 285, 287-288
Jenne, David	796	D	D: 32	L: 56, 68, 82-84, 278, 297-298
Jett, John	430	D	C: 48-49	G: 566, 575-576, 580, 649, 656; H: 101-102, 207, K: 403-404, 414
Jewell, George C.	230	D	B: 405-406, 447-448, 521-522, 625-626	F: 72, 102, 125, 159, 199, 213, 302, 328, 349-350, 355, 373, 386-387, 396, 397, 406, 576, 587, 595, 596, 602, 604-606, 629, 637, 641, 656, 668
Jewell, Jesse	516	D	C: 238-239, 268-269	H: 539, 559, 564-565; I: 110; J: 58-59, 89, 98, 104-105, 600-601, 639; K: 4, 16, 30-31; L: 165-167
Jewell, Mary	715	D	C: 690-691	J: 624-625, 629, 639; K: 13, 16, 30, 58, 110; O: 496
Johnson, Charles	122	M	A: 136; B: 617-618, 647-648	D: 220, 232, 339; F: 616, 626, 637, 644, 656, 661, 695, 719
Johnson, George W.	56	D	A: 68-69	B: 428, 429; C: 3, 5, 10; D: 30, 34, 90; D: 217, 220, 221, 230, 249, 258, 271
Johnson, James G.	1010	D	D: 256	O: 183-184, 212-213, 232, 235, 236, 260, 388, 399, 425-428, 433

Name	File #	Type	Fee Book & Register	Minute Book
Johnson, Levi	787	D	D: 23	L: 5, 27-29, 36, 420-421, 454, 465-466, 558-559; M: 6-10
Johnson, Melville	886	D	D: 126	M: 144, 163, 171, 203; O: 278, 298-299
Johnson, Thomas J.	465	D	C: 126-127	H: 192, 204, 205-206, 214-215, 224-225; L: 129-130
Johnson, William	1053	D	D: 300	O: 516-517
Johnson, William Alonzo	122	M	A: 136; B: 617-618, 647-648	D: 220, 232, 339; F: 616, 626, 637, 644, 656, 661, 695, 719; G: 581, 584-585; H: 27
Johnson, William B.	94	D	A: 107-108	D: 51, 71-72, 107, 108, 147-148, 208-209, 304, 313, 335, 342, 349, 366
Jones, A. J.	372	D	B: 781-782	G: 217-218, 396, 423-425, 433, 476-478, 519
Jones, Fred	623	M	C: 490-491	J: 42-43
Jones, Mary	890	D	D: 130	M: 201-202, 231, 239, 376-377, 443-445, 614-616; N: 24-25, 44, 74, 94-96
Jones, Minnie	623	M	C: 490-491	J: 42-43
Jones, William	119	D	A: 135	D: 217, 221
Jones, Williard D.	613	D	C: 466-467	I: 585
Joost, John	948	D	D: 192	N: 188-189, 227-229, 249-250, 293, 421-422, 489-496; O: 53, 67-68, 222-223, 239-241
Jordan, Joshua	642	D	C: 528-529	J: 162, 210-212, 315; K: 213, 219-221
Jordan, William H.	785	D	D: 21	K: 454; L: 12-13, 18-20, 217-218, 233, 263, 264-265
Joyce, Ann	618	D	C: 478-479	J: 12-13, 37-38, 49, 81, 432, 495, 517, 601, 602; K: 370, 384, 385; M: 20-21
Joyce, Thomas	920	D	D: 160	M: 483-484, 550, 565-566, 588; N: 622-623, 631; O: 20, 73
Judkins, L. M.	100	I	A: 113	D: 91, 92, 115
Keithly, Jacob	763	D	C: 796-797; D: 104	K: 296, 318-320, 328-329; L: 269-270, 427, 483-487, 625-626; M: 20, 27-29; N: 83, 113, 230-232, 233, 311-317, 417, 477-478, 568-570, 621-622; O: 5, 40-45, 359
Kellogg, Warren S.	619	D	C: 480-481	J: 21-22, 44-46, 637; K: 7-9
Kelly, Michael	528	D	C: 264-265	H: 574; I: 431

Name	File #	Type	Fee Book & Register	Minute Book
Kelsey, Joseph	57	M	A: 70; B: 731	B: 109, 112, 116-117, 119-120, 130-131, 141-142; G: 102
Kelsey, William	57	M	A: 70; B: 731	B: 109, 112, 116-117, 119-120, 130-131, 141-142; G: 102
Kelty, Anna L.	729	M	C: 720-721	K: 84-85, 86
Kemp, Thomas	831	D	D: 69	L: 343, 381-383, 384, 386; M: 34-36, 68-70, 87
Kennedy, Hugh C.	751	D	C: 768-769	K: 223, 235; L: 224-225, 281-282, 368, 435-436; M: 57, 424, 451, 494, 495-497
Kenny, Patrick	979	I	D: 224	N: 601-602, 620
Kern, George	59	D	A: 73	B: 414, 425; C: 2, 6-7; D: 163, 188, 196, 204, 215, 226, 229
Kidd, Peleg	277	D	B: 559-560, 825-826	F: 470, 475-476, 507-508, 515-516, 669, 764, 772-773; G: 230-233, 298, 378, 387, 400, 543, 565, 613, 633, 643-646; H: 81-82, 100, 109-111, 119-120, 122
Kiernan, Michael	664	D	C: 580-581	J: 316, 324, 335-336, 350-351
Kimball, Ada P.	922	M	D: 162	M: 581-582, 628-629
Kimball, George Washington	845	D	D: 84	L: 487-488, 503, 535, 536, 541-543; M: 439, 492, 533-534, 583; N: 66, 342, 554, 577; O: 79, 255, 265, 283, 300, 321, 340, 396, 405, 421
Kimball, Georgie	922	M	D: 162	M: 581-582, 628-629
Kimball, Helen M.	922	M	D: 162	M: 581-582, 628-629
Kimball, J. T.	287	D	B: 579-580	F: 532, 544
Kimball, Lelia M.	922	M	D: 162	M: 581-582, 628-629
Kimball, Sarah Ann	921	D	D: 161	M: 491-492, 534-535, 582; N: 66
Kincaid, Oscar F.	789	M	D: 25	L: 6, 11
King, Alice	924	M	D: 164	M: 460; O: 141-142, 169, 174
King, Jessie	923	D	D: 163	M: 430, 511, 553-554, 596; N: 86-87, 159-160, 613-614, 632; O: 1-4
King, Samuel	924	M	D: 164	M: 460; O: 141-142, 169, 174
Kirk, Alice J.	112	M	A: 129	D: 150, 159
Kiser/Kizer, Abraham Cooper	776	M	D: 12	M: 63
Kiser/Kizer, Henrietta	776	M	D: 12	M: 63
Kiser/Kizer, John P.	776	D	D: 12	K: 360, 389; L: 384, 425-426, 506, 524, 578, 610, 621-623; M: 39
Klink, George E.	499	M	C: 196-197	H: 377

Name	File #	Type	Fee Book & Register	Minute Book
Klink, Margaret J.	499	M	C: 196-197	H: 377
Klink, Nicholas Ward	499	M	C: 196-197	H: 377
Knaak, August	853	D	D: 92	L: 536, 551-552, 566-567, 628-629; M: 65, 92-93, 136, 197, 207-209, 295, 509, 575; N: 173-174, 183-186
Knight, George	967	M	D: 211	N: 496-497, 500-501
Koger/Kougar, William	58	D	A: 71-72	B: 210, 215, 223-224, 257, 384, 394, 410-411; D: 26, 89, 267, 328, 331, 337-338, 339
Kolmer, Josepha	274	D	B: 551-552	F: 449, 466, 526, 669, 672, 682-684
Kron, John	862	D	D: 102	L: 612, 633-634; M: 24, 115-116, 244; N: 406, 433, 466-470
Lallement, Jean Nicholas	1049	D	D: 296	O: 497-498
Lamb, Horace	359	D	B: 753-754; C: 44-45	G: 133, 144, 169, 172, 357, 372, 375, 379-383, 409-411, 556, 562, 585-588, 613, 624-625
Lambert, Selvenus/Sylvanus/Silvanus D.	244	D	B: 461-462; C: 394-395	F: 230, 236, 237-238, 242, 248, 255, 282-283, 446, 449, 458, 482, 566, 676-677, 689, 696, 704; I: 367
Lambkins/Lampkins/Lamkins, James L.	172	D	B: 133-134, 281-282	E: 195, 206, 428, 448-449, 466, 469, 485, 510, 519-520
Lamkin, A. A.	883	D	D: 122	M: 119, 156, 172, 175, 237-238, 294, 327-328; N: 98-99
Lamott, William H.	854	D	D: 93	L: 545, 549-550; M: 2
Lamphere, Charles	388	D	B: 811-812	G: 274, 281, 313, 322, 338, 339, 544-545
Lane, John D.	566	D	C: 360-361	I: 248, 280, 290-291, 292, 311-312, 313, 341; J: 349, 451-452, 477-478
Langdon, Eliza Jane	1046	D	D: 293	O: 469, 472-473, 486, 487, 516
Langer, Henry	741	D	C: 744-745	K: 155-156
LaPlant, Casimere	1047	D	D: 294	O: 484, 514
Larsen, Olef	401	D	B: 837-838; C: 382-383	G: 357-358, 360, 475, 647; H: 13-14, 235, 261, 273, 280; I: 255-256, 276-277, 304, 327, 355, 523-524, 586; J: 16, 240-241, 248, 265-268, 400, 424-426, 433-434
Lashley, Elizabeth (aka Findley, Elizabeth)	584	M	C: 404-405	I: 405-406, 475-476; O: 365, 382-383

Name	File #	Type	Fee Book & Register	Minute Book
Lassins, Christian	973	D	D: 217	N: 542, 552, 560, 570-571, 586, 598; O: 66-67, 72, 127, 135-138, 178, 207-208, 278, 291-292
Latapie, Edward	1044	D	D: 291	O: 467-468, 491, 504-505, 517-518, 519, 523-526
Laufenberger/Laufenburg, Mary	271	I	B: 545-546	F: 445, 450
Laufenberger/Laufenburger, Philip	394	D	B: 823-824	G: 289, 293, 301, 304, 309
Laufenburger, Phillipp	595	D	C: 430-431	I: 498, 513-514
Lawlor/Lawler, James	791	D	D: 27	L: 22-23, 66, 87, 112; M: 137, 169, 225-227
Lawrence, R. M.	311	D	B: 641-642	F: 673, 677; G: 55, 62-63
Lawton, John W.	575	D	C: 380-381	I: 326, 331-332, 335, 358-359, 382; J: 255, 294-298, 369-370
Leak, Charles W.	526	M	C: 260-261	H: 573-574, 577-578; I: 414, 457, 468-470
Leak, John D.	526	M	C: 260-261	H: 573-574, 577-578; I: 414, 457, 468-470; K: 93, 110-111; N: 526-527
Leard, Robert A.	617	D	C: 474-475	J: 11-12, 35-37, 162; K: 188, 189
Leary, James	638	D	C: 520-521	J: 121, 142-144, 175, 206-207, 533-534, 579
Leavenworth, James D.	61	D	A: 72	B: 234
Ledwidge, John	469	D	C: 136-137	H: 227, 231, 233, 235, 477, 501; L: 125-126
Lees, William	258	D	B: 503-504	F: 343; G: 38, 49, 67, 68, 73-77; G: 291, 505, 537, 545, 553-554
Lees, William	367	D	B: 771-772	G: 191, 200, 305, 312-313
Legendre, Lewis	18	D	A: 19	B: 143-144, 159-160
Leigh, Barton	810	D	D: 48	L: 143, 170-171, 181, 195, 217
Leihy, George W.	331	D	B: 691-692	F: 797, 802; G: 31, 35, 36, 535; H: 438; I: 334, 361-364, 388-389; N: 606-607
Lennox, John	115	D	A: 132; B: 157-158	D: 177, 186, 282, 296, 309; E: 18, 19, 240, 244-245; F: 539, 542, 554-556
Leonard, Charles W.	978	I	D: 223	N: 601, 617-618; O: 37, 66, 110-112, 139-140, 194, 378
Levens, Charles	259	D	B: 505-506	F: 352
Levy, Louis	512	D	C: 230-231	H: 510, 526-527, 530

Name	File #	Type	Fee Book & Register	Minute Book
Levy, Seligman	555	D	C: 338-339	I: 168, 186, 187, 206-207, 216, 273, 282-284, 295-296, 337-339, 465; J: 521, 536-540, 545-546
Lewis, George	22	M	A: 23; B: 821-822	D: 257, 275, 300, 304, 314-315, 371, 376-377; G: 395, 416-420
Lewis, George W.	60	D	A: 74-75	B: 136, 139, 142, 150-151, 259, 277-280
Lewis, Jasper N.	631	D	C: 506-507	J: 98, 109, 115, 122, 201-202, 320, 339-341
Lewis, John	21	D	A: 22	B: 83, 86-88, 89-92, 93, 98, 105
Lewis, John	22	M	A: 23; B: 821-822	D: 257, 275, 300, 304, 314-315, 371, 376-377; G: 395, 416-420, 437, 456-457
Lewis, Joseph	22	M	A: 23; B: 821-822	D: 257, 275, 300, 304, 314-315, 371, 376-377; G: 395, 416-420, 437, 456-457
Lewis, Joshua H.	382	D	B: 799-800	G: 242, 255
Lewis, Leanna	60	M	A: 74-75	B: 158; D: 70-71
Lewis, Maria	22	M	A: 23; B: 821-822	D: 257, 275, 300, 304, 314-315, 371, 376-377; G: 395, 416-420
Lewis, Nevill/Nevile/Neville	60	M	A: 74-75	B: 158; D: 70-71
Lewis, Sophia	22	M	A: 23; B: 821-822	D: 257, 275, 300, 304, 314-315, 371, 376-377; G: 395, 416-420
Lewis, Sylvester	60	M	A: 74-75	B: 158; D: 70-71
Liddle, Hugh	809	D	D: 47	L: 144, 162, 179-180, 211, 235-236
Liddle, Lucinda	814	M	D: 52	L: 162-164, 395-396, 416-417; M: 417, 433, 455-457, 560, 577
Liddle, Nancy	806	D	D: 44	L: 136, 151-152, 153, 164-165
Lind, Emma	473	M	C: 144-145	H: 238
Lindsey, Thomas S.	371	D	B: 779-780	G: 203, 256
Linus, John	245	D	B: 463-464	F: 231, 245, 262, 668, 685-687, 704-705; G: 32-33
Little, Thomas C.	636	D	C: 516-517	J: 119-120, 144-145, 248, 349, 361-363
Littlefield, Edward E.	1034	M	D: 281	O: 404, 423, 438-439
Littlefield, Emma G.	1034	M	D: 281	O: 404, 423, 438-439
Littlefield, Rosie C.	1034	M	D: 281	O: 404, 423, 438-439
Littlefield, Warren A.	1034	M	D: 281	O: 404, 423, 438-439
Long, William	695	D	C: 648-649	J: 495-496, 515-516, 519-520, 551, 609-610; K: 380, 390-391

Name	File #	Type	Fee Book & Register	Minute Book
Lovejoy, Mary Grove/Gould	666	D	C: 584-585	J: 323, 351-352
Lowell, Samuel D.	191	D	B: 227-228	E: 348, 361-362
Lowery, Benjamin	926	M	D: 166	N: 85-86, 106
Lowery, William	926	M	D: 166	N: 85-86, 106
Lowery/Lowry, Eliza	954	D	D: 198	N: 272-273, 304-305, 306, 378, 636, 637; O: 12-15
Lowry/Lowery, William	363	D	B: 763-764	G: 170, 177, 356, 358-359, 390-391, 399, 523, 546, 548-550, 591, 599-601
Lucas, John	593	D	C: 424-425	I: 477-478, 494-496, 523, 565-566
Lynch, Michael	925	D	D: 165	M: 477, 522, 523; O: 483, 508, 522
Lynch, William	591	D	C: 418-419	I: 470-471, 497-498
Lyon, Albert G.	1002	D	D: 247	O: 123, 154-155, 174-175
Lyon, James J.	302	D	B: 613-614; C: 70-71	F: 615, 621-622, 628, 632, 649, 748; G: 100, 113-114, 119, 140-141, 143-144, 156, 157-158, 180-181; H: 277-278; K: 224, 240-241; L: 413-415; N: 290-291
Lyons, William	180	D	B: 169-170, 307-308, 387-388	E: 257, 273, 287, 292, 293, 309, 312-313, 498, 517, 527, 528, 536, 611, 625; F: 4, 17, 42, 55, 69, 73, 108, 121-122
Lyster, Mary	904	D	D: 144	M: 362, 368-369, 394-395
Lytaker, John T.	352	M	B: 739-740	G: 105-106, 117
Macken/Mackin, Robert	995	M	D: 240	O: 83-84, 85-86
Macy, Theora	194	M		E: 458; G: 228-229; J: 138, 192-194, 226-228
Macy, Vesta S.	392	D	B: 819-820; C: 6-7, 284-285	G: 290, 296, 297, 304, 319, 415, 429-430; H: 35, 39, 130; I: 14-15, 162-163, 194-195, 196
Macy, William M.	194	D	B: 239-240, 293-294, 345-346	E: 380, 395, 412, 414, 451, 457, 458, 470, 482, 483-484, 548-549, 570, 572-575, 594, 595-597
Madler, Anna F.	605	M	C: 450-451	I: 528-529
Madler, Clara J.	605	M	C: 450-451	I: 528-529
Madler, Elizabeth M.	605	M	C: 450-451	I: 528-529
Madler, Margretta	605	M	C: 450-451	I: 528-529
Madler, Stephen	492	D	C: 182-183, 334-335	H: 356-357, 371, 372-373, 388, 426, 432-433, 476-477, 504, 564; I: 437-438, 447-451

Name	File #	Type	Fee Book & Register	Minute Book
Magoun/Magoon, Samuel C.	876	D	D: 115	M: 72, 93-95, 114, 222, 441-442, 488-491; N: 201
Mallen, Edward	1000	D	D: 245	O: 114, 126, 156, 175-176, 192, 217-218, 231, 350
Mann, John	569	D	C: 368-369	I: 271, 285, 356-357; J: 231
Mansfield, Lynus	413	D	C: 16-17	G: 444, 461, 473-475, 499-500, 509, 510; H: 42-43, 78-79, 132, 176, 193, 213-214
Mantle, William	116	D	A: 131; B: 119-120, 275-276	D: 183, 203, 208, 245, 259; E: 174, 189, 204, 209, 234, 259, 284, 299, 316, 323, 345, 360, 373-374, 417, 431, 449-450
Marr, George H.	944	D	D: 188	N: 183, 209, 224-225, 226, 235, 251-253, 274-276, 498-499, 578, 590, 591-594, 612-613
Marrs, A. B.	846	D	D: 85	L: 489-490, 505-506, 547-548, 554-555, 560, 580-581; M: 23-24, 67-68; N: 325, 346-347, 360; O: 9-10, 36-37
Marsh, H.	263	D	B: 523-524	F: 389, 393, 395, 519, 592, 627, 638, 643, 654
Marsharie, Martin	118	D	A: 134; B: 27-28, 137-138	D: 207, 218, 222, 223, 225, 229, 235, 276, 308, 320, 326; E: 45, 56-57, 182, 212, 221, 237-238
Martin, Richard Montgomery	624	D	C: 492-493	J: 43, 71-73, 163, 171-172, 581, 604-606
Mast, Francis Xavier	268	D	B: 539-540	F: 438, 449, 468, 498, 508; G: 363, 369, 648, 655-656; H: 22, 44, 47-49, 65-67, 245, 272, 274-275
Matheson, George G.	222	M		F: 717, 748, 752, 790; G: 4, 5-6, 31-32
Matheson, Nettie	222	M		F: 717, 748, 752, 790; G: 4, 5-6, 31-32
Matheson, Roderick	222	M		F: 717, 748, 752, 790; G: 4, 5-6, 31-32
Matheson, Roderick N.	222	D	B: 377-378	F: 14, 22, 37, 722
Mathews, Sarah E.	279	D	B: 563-564	F: 474, 495, 500, 501, 502, 673, 678-679; G: 63
Matthews, Charles W., Jr.	423	M	C: 34-35	G: 527-528, 542-543
Matthews, McKenny	242	D		

Name	File #	Type	Fee Book & Register	Minute Book
Matthews, Overton B.	802	D	D: 38	L: 85, 97, 113, 184; M: 290, 381, 382, 420-421; N: 79, 118-121; O: 367, 409, 430-432, 443, 462, 475-476
Maupin, Richard A.	104	D	A: 119-120	D: 101, 121, 145, 149, 161, 254, 260, 269, 309, 318-319
Maxwell, John M.	678	D	C: 614-615	J: 417, 459-460, 467; K: 259-260, 309, 339-341, 358, 400, 410
Mayhew, Edwin (Capt.)	144	D	A: 158; B: 19-20	E: 2, 4, 9, 125, 213, 222, 235-237, 405
McCaskie, Galbraith	894	D	D: 134	M: 234, 241-242, 251-252; N: 144-145, 151, 164-165
McChristian, James Washington	818	D	D: 56	L: 211-212, 233-235
McChristian, Maria	892	D	D: 132	M: 223, 240-241, 282-284, 368; N: 629-630; O: 8
McClish, John N.	321	M	B: 667-668	F: 739, 744-745
McCluskey, John	1019	D	D: 266	O: 309, 325-326, 331, 351, 398
McCluskey, John H.	984	D	D: 229	N: 635; O: 20-21, 27-28, 74, 81-82, 226-227, 228-230
McCorkle, Aria T.	971	D	D: 215	N: 524, 538, 545, 549-550, 564, 565; O: 219
McCracken, Emma	949	M	D: 193	N: 222-223
McCracken, George F.	949	M	D: 193	N: 222-223
McCracken, Jared P.	111	D	A: 128	D: 150, 160, 203, 245
McCracken, John C.	434	D	C: 56-57, 272-273	G: 615, 630-631, 654; H: 45, 52-54, 59-60, 64, 81, 127, 144-146, 159, 233, 258, 272, 284, 292-293, 576, 595; I: 20-22, 25, 129-136, 257-261, 458-459
McCullough, David A.	503	M	C: 204-205	H: 446
McCullough, Mary L.	503	M	C: 204-205	H: 446
McCurdy, John	201	D	B: 273-274	E: 427, 443, 451-452, 481
McDonell/McDonald, Angus	871	D	D: 112	M: 45-46, 65, 95, 96, 102, 117, 449, 492-493, 622-623
McFarland, Garret	65	D	A: 78	B: 410, 416
McGee, Robert	490	I	C: 176-177; D: 219	H: 322-323, 337; K: 179, 210-211, 262, 330-331, 449; N: 276-277, 295-297, 319-320, 376-377, 401-402, 433-439, 484, 525, 545-546, 547, 559-560, 580; O: 30-31, 89-90
McGinty, Daniel	496	D	C: 190-191	H: 398, 419-420, 423, 492
McGuire, Cora E.	866	M	D: 106	L: 630; M: 306, 325, 468-470

Name	File #	Type	Fee Book & Register	Minute Book
McGuire, William C.	420	D	C: 28-29	G: 501, 524, 525
McKinnon, William W.	113	D	A: 129	D: 158, 175
McKnight, William	12	D	A: 13	B: 143-144, 157
McLaughlin, Hugh	197	D	B: 249-250, 469-470	E: 406, 416, 426, 430, 454, 552, 554-555; F: 239, 252, 266, 277, 310, 374, 404, 410; G: 48, 49, 104, 118, 256, 268, 269-270, 276-277
McLaughlin, Mary Grace	197	M		H: 481
McMinn, Charles V.	931	M	D: 171	M: 397, 564
McMinn, Joseph A.	931	M	D: 171	M: 397, 564
McMinn, Joseph, Jr.	289	D	B: 583-584, 823	F: 532, 538, 546, 574, 581; H: 476, 492-493, 498; I: 209, 244-246; K: 399; L: 490, 508, 518, 520-521; M: 446, 498-501, 544-547, 563-564
McMinn, Mary F.	931	M	D: 171	M: 397, 564
McNamara, Harriet	900	D	D: 140	M: 266, 291, 306, 308-309, 328-329, 367, 384, 385, 391, 608-609; O: 101-102, 116, 121, 138, 148, 198
McPeak, Matthew	646	D	C: 536-537	J: 176, 207-208, 213, 224, 261-262; M: 626-628; N: 26, 50-55
McPherson, Annie E.	778	M	D: 14	K: 406-407; N: 99, 187, 221-222, 586, 594-596
McPherson, Charles Perry	740	D	C: 742-743; D: 82	K: 151-152, 180-182, 190-191, 203-204, 242-243, 247, 287-290; L: 1, 11, 29-30, 117, 134-136, 155, 191, 192, 195-201, 543-544
McPherson, Delana/Dulana	778	M	D: 14	K: 406-407; L: 469-470
McPherson, Donald	199	D	B: 263-264, 295-296	E: 423, 433, 455, 456, 462; F: 16, 25-26, 40, 55, 76-77
McPherson, Early	778	M	D: 14	K: 406-407; N: 99, 187, 221-222, 586, 594-596
McPherson, Ewell	778	M	D: 14	K: 406-407; N: 99, 187, 221-222, 586, 594-596
McPherson, French	778	M	D: 14	K: 406-407; N: 99, 187, 221-222, 586, 594-596
McPherson, Mary E.	778	M	D: 14	K: 406-407; N: 99, 187, 221-222, 586, 594-596
McPherson, Miller	778	M	D: 14	K: 406-407; L: 544-545
McPherson, Stonewall	778	M	D: 14	K: 406-407; N: 99, 187, 221-222, 586, 594-596

Name	File #	Type	Fee Book & Register	Minute Book
McPherson, Thomas Welcome	1036	D	D: 283	O: 424, 451, 452-453
McReynolds, Jacob	699	D	C: 656-657	J: 524, 559-560, 638; K: 42-43; O: 69, 86, 157-160, 315-316, 329, 338-340, 369, 370-372
McReynolds, Stephen	429	D	C: 46-47	G: 555, 562-563, 569, 574-575
Mead, Alice C.	725	M	C: 712-713	K: 26-27, 40-41, 43-47, 88, 101-103
Mead, Catherine C.	759	D	C: 786-787	K: 268-269, 300-301, 344-346, 383-384; M: 292-293, 361-362
Mead, William	370	D	B: 777-778	G: 203, 209, 211, 236, 243-244, 339-341, 398-399, 526, 533-534
Medley, Anderville G.	841	D	D: 79	L: 441, 471-473, 638-639; N: 179
Meeker, Clementina S.	383	M		G: 275
Meeker, Estella	383	M		G: 275
Meeker, Orion S.	383	M		G: 275
Meeker, Sarah	383	D	B: 801-802	G: 250, 257
Melton, Clymina	1006	M	D: 251	O: 150
Melton, Jacob Newton	329	M	B: 687-688	F: 793, 800-801
Melton, James Benjamin	1006	M	D: 251	O: 150
Melton, John Nelson	329	M	B: 687-688	F: 793, 800-801
Melton, Mary Catharine	329	M	B: 687-688	F: 793, 800-801
Melton, Robert Wilson	1006	M	D: 251	O: 150
Melton, William	869	D	D: 109, 253	L: 637-638; M: 14-17, 89, 292, 329-330, 472-473, 634, 637; N: 75-76, 89-91, 116-118; O: 142-143, 148-149, 172-174, 432, 436, 447-448
Melton, William Woodson	1006	M	D: 251	O: 150
Menefee, James R.	110	D	A: 127-128; B: 21-22, 123-124, 229-230	D: 137, 152, 156, 162, 233, 236, 240, 264, 280, 282, 295, 345-346, 379; E: 2, 5, 41, 48, 68, 77-78, 139-140, 160, 175, 184, 208-209, 243, 258, 263-264, 327, 345, 353-355
Menefee, Sarah Jane	341	I	B: 711-712, 849-850	G: 62, 78-79, 443-444, 455; H: 59, 67-68; I: 379, 402-404; K: 153, 175, 176; M: 201, 235, 256-257
Merchant, Frederick	1035	M	D: 282	O: 404, 423, 439
Merritt, Charles	805	D	D: 43	L: 133, 142, 162, 173-174; O: 100-101
Mertens, Christian	241	D	B: 457-458	F: 229, 246, 314, 351-352, 390, 395, 444, 546, 564, 565

Name	File #	Type	Fee Book & Register	Minute Book
Messenger, Charles H.	813	D	D: 51	L: 147-148, 161, 190-191, 327, 362-363
Metcalf, Amanda	665	M	C: 582-583	J: 319-320; L: 156, 174-176; M: 282, 306-307; N: 297, 327; O: 26, 65
Meyer, Augusta	621	M	C: 486-487	J: 33
Meyer, Frederick	620	M	C:484-485	J: 33, 35
Meyer, Julia	621	M	C: 486-487	J: 33
Meyer, Katy/Katie	621	M	C: 486-487	J: 33
Meyer, William	508	D	C: 220-221	H: 503, 522-523, 533-534; I: 439-440, 471-474; J: 321
Meyer, William	621	M	C: 486-487	J: 33
Middleton, L. A.	930	D	D: 170	N: 151, 157-158, 159, 403-404, 427, 428-431
Middleton, Walter V.	532	M	C: 276-277	I: 12; L: 291, 365, 452-453, 458, 467, 471, 475
Middleton, William H.	556	D	C: 340-341	I: 174-175, 225-226, 248-249, 274, 277-278, 339; J: 410, 454-456, 616-618
Middleton, William W.	195	D	B: 241-242	E: 380, 388-389, 396
Miears/Mier/Meirer/Meyer, John	255	D	B: 495-496	F: 306, 324-325, 332, 524, 545, 552, 561-562
Miles, John	312	D	B: 643-644, 717-718	F: 674, 693, 705, 757, 765; G: 77-78, 86-87, 99
Millar, Joseph Morgan	728	D	C: 718-719	K: 74-75, 95-97, 104, 442-443, 449-454, 461-462
Miller, Amelia/Armelia M.	928	M	D: 168	M: 636-637; N: 37-38
Miller, Charles	774	D	D: 10	K: 375-376, 385-386, 415, 419-420; L: 21, 42-43, 207, 222-223, 241-242, 253-255
Miller, Daniel	66	D	A: 79-80	B: 295, 306, 312, 329, 332-334, 335-336, 342-343, 347, 368-370, 389, 413, 421-422, 425-426; D: 28, 38, 42, 46, 53, 59-60, 66, 77, 79, 84, 87, 96, 97, 98-99, 192
Miller, Daniel E.	135	M	A: 148; B: 11-12, 455-456	D: 28, 88, 370; E: 30, 36, 41, 42, 418; F: 65, 177, 181, 185, 202-203, 228, 267, 293
Miller, Edmond/Edmund/Edward H.	120	M	A: 135; B: 755-756	D: 218-219; G: 134, 148-149

Name	File #	Type	Fee Book & Register	Minute Book
Miller, Frederick H.	940	M	D: 182	M: 218-219, 580
Miller, George E.	940	M	D: 182	M: 218-219, 580
Miller, George K.	88	M	A: 100	D: 28, 88
Miller, George W.	63	D	A: 77	B: 146, 148, 154, 155, 162, 164, 165, 295, 309-310, 318-319
Miller, Greenberry/Greenbury	734	D	C: 730-731	K: 119, 138, 142-143, 144-145; L: 31-32, 410-411; N: 589, 600, 620
Miller, James R.	928	M	D: 168	M: 636-637; N: 37-38
Miller, Joseph H.	24	D	A: 25	B: 63-65
Miller, L. W.	783	D	D: 19	K: 429, 446, 447-448; L: 14-15, 45, 53-54, 86-87; M: 158-159, 160-161, 179, 186, 209, 214-218, 580, 581
Miller, Lewis	1031	M	D: 278	O: 410, 411-412
Miller, Mary Ann	136	M	A: 149-150	D: 28, 63, 88, 95, 105, 291, 302, 306, 307, 312, 321, 336, 367, 370, 371, 380; E: 10, 30, 33
Miller, Mary J.	928	M	D: 168	M: 636-637; N: 37-38
Miller, Mary Jane	120	M	A: 135; B: 755-756	D: 218-219; G: 134, 148-149
Miller, Nannie E.	928	M	D: 168	M: 636-637; N: 37-38
Miller, Rachel	928	M	D: 168	M: 636-637; N: 37-38
Miller, Robert B.	454	D	C: 102-103	H: 99, 114, 125-126, 127, 131, 137, 138, 170-171, 271, 431, 440-442, 478-479
Miller, Samuel	189	D	B: 221-222, 257-258	E: 330, 359-360, 365, 416-417, 422, 432, 525, 527, 533-534, 540, 546-547
Miller, Samuel E.	868	D	D: 108	L: 631-632; M: 11-12, 46, 47, 62, 341-342, 353-354, 609-610, 635-636; N: 29, 30, 31-35
Miller, Sarah A.	928	M	D: 168	M: 636-637
Miller, Saul	868½	D	D: 108	N: 66, 121-122, 474-475, 489, 505-506, 512
Miller, Valentine	354	I	B: 743-744	G: 124, 128-129, 132, 147, 172-173, 176, 188-190, 247, 272, 294-295, 337, 408, 415, 435-436
Millington, Anna Electa	730	M	C: 722-723	K: 90, 97-98, 120, 145, 165
Millington, Buchanan	730	M	C: 722-723	K: 90, 97-98, 120, 145, 165
Millington, John	730	M	C: 722-723	K: 90, 97-98, 120, 145, 165

Name	File #	Type	Fee Book & Register	Minute Book
Millington, Seth	339	D	B: 707-708	G: 51-52, 65, 109, 114-115, 118, 169, 173-174, 199; I: 25-27
Millington, Seth	730	M	C: 722-723	K: 90, 97-98, 120, 145, 165
Millington, Zachariah	730	M	C: 722-723	K: 90, 97-98, 120, 145, 165
Mills, Niles	717	D	C: 696-697	J: 631; K: 6-7, 135, 265-266, 416-418
Miner, Welcome E.	690	D	C: 638-639; D: 110	J: 482, 490-492, 544-545; K: 58-59, 422, 423, 428, 435-436, 437; L: 33, 424, 442, 571-572, 584-585, 591, 623-624; M: 5, 107, 122, 253, 289, 407-409
Mingus, Peter	929	I	D: 169	N: 141, 149-150
Minkel, Henry	1005	D	D: 250	O: 141, 161-162, 177, 190, 204-205, 206, 262, 282, 453, 474, 503-504
Mitchell, Benjamin H.	433	D	C: 54-55, 292-293	G: 621, 632, 650; H: 46, 106-107, 207-208, 219, 241; I: 48, 59-61, 68-69, 389-390
Mize, Merrill	731	D	C: 724-725	K: 94, 127-129, 171
Mizer, Henry Clay	941	D	D: 184	N: 41-42, 68-69, 70, 73-74, 156-157; O: 97-99, 280-281, 287, 324-325, 428-429, 433-434, 435, 445-446, 455, 458-459, 494-496
Mock, John L.	990	D	D: 235	O: 38, 71, 112, 119, 163-164, 243, 257
Molloy, Edward B.	476	D	C: 152-153	H: 245, 268-269, 279, 313, 341-342, 350, 370, 411-413; I: 202, 244, 246-247, 513, 567-571
Money, C. C.	285	D	B: 575-576	F: 516
Montevon/Montevan, George	452	D	C: 98-99	H: 95, 101
Moore, Charles	330	M	B: 689-690	F: 795-796, 801; H: 504, 531-532
Moore, Charles	790½	M	D: 26	L: 16-17
Moore, Charles	1004	M	D: 249	O: 134, 142, 151, 156, 207, 253-254, 292-293, 304-305
Moore, Elijah		M		B: 314
Moore, Elisha	295	D	B: 597-598	F: 549-550, 568, 575-576, 584, 592-594, 787, 794-795, 796; H: 531-532
Moore, Elizabeth Ellen	330	M	B: 689-690	F: 795-796, 801; H: 504, 531-532
Moore, Francis M.	330	M	B: 689-690	F: 795-796, 801; H: 504, 531-532

Name	File #	Type	Fee Book & Register	Minute Book
Moore, George O. (also O'Moore, George)	543	D	C: 302-303	I: 79-80, 114-115, 585-586; J: 159-161, 223; M: 169, 192, 193-194, 430-431, 461-463
Moore, Henrietta	330	M	B: 689-690	F: 795-796, 801; H: 504, 531-532
Moore, Henrietta	790½	M	D: 26	L: 16-17
Moore, Henrietta	1004	M	D: 249	O: 134, 142, 151, 156, 207, 253-254, 292-293, 304-305
Moore, Henry		M		B: 314
Moore, Laura	330	M	B: 689-690	F: 795-796, 801; H: 504, 531-532
Moore, Laura A.	790½	M	D: 26	L: 16-17
Moore, Lydia	1038	D	D: 285	O: 456-457, 473-474, 480, 489
Moore, Mary E.	509	M	C: 224-225	
Moore, Nancy Celia		M		B: 314
Moore, Patrick	839	D	D: 77	L: 409, 436-437, 457; M: 40, 390-391, 398, 427, 452-453
Moore, Perry	330	M	B: 689-690	F: 795-796, 801; H: 504, 531-532
Moore, William T.	586	M	C: 408-409	I: 424
Morgan, Charles	334	D	B: 697-698	G: 13, 18, 21, 91, 110
Morgan, Robert D.	927	D	D: 167	M: 482-483, 527-528, 529, 610-611; N: 9-12
Morrison, Thomas	895	D	D: 135	M: 237, 270, 281, 414-415, 485-486; N: 135, 145-147
Morrison/Morison, Melinda	1045	D	D: 292	O: 468, 491, 499-500, 511
Morse, Susan B.	519	D	C: 244-245	H: 557; M: 44-45, 93, 124-126, 454
Mountjoy, Lula F.	770	M	D: 6	K: 336
Mulgrew, Felix	830	D	D: 68	L: 311-312, 332-333, 505, 604, 616
Munday, Alice	684	M	C: 626-627	J: 446-447
Munday, B. B.	626	D	C: 496-497	J: 51, 63-64, 146-148, 587-589, 612, 620-622; K: 23-24, 60-62, 63-64, 65
Munday, C. F.	684	M	C: 626-627	J: 446-447
Munday, Fanny	684	M	C: 626-627	J: 446-447
Munday, M. E. C.	684	M	C: 626-627	J: 446-447
Mundy, Amanda	64	M	A: 74	B: 200, 201-202, 298
Mundy, Thomas	64	M	A: 74	B: 200, 201-202, 298
Murphy, Patrick	1041	D	D: 288	O: 459-460, 487-489
Murray, John O.	169	D	B: 117-118, 233-234	E: 171, 178, 276, 302-303, 338-339, 366
Murray, Mary Alice	106	M	A: 95	D: 110, 124

Name	File #	Type	Fee Book & Register	Minute Book
Nason, John M.	475	M	C: 150-151	H: 262; J: 260-261, 277-278, 298, 317-318, 631; K: 23; M: 185, 186, 274-276, 279, 584, 606-608; N: 206-207, 253-254, 294, 310, 396-398, 399
Nason, Mary Emma	475	M	C: 150-151	H: 262; J: 260-261, 277-278, 298, 317-318, 631; K: 23; M: 185, 186, 274-276, 279, 584, 606-608; N: 206-207, 253-254, 294, 310, 396-398, 399
Nauyokes/Nauyoks, Charles	786	D	D: 22	K: 455; L: 13, 17-18, 26, 54, 324-325, 362, 371-372
Neeb, Johanna	480	D	C: 160-161	H: 290, 306, 307; I: 64-65, 421-422, 444-446, 455-456, 461-464
Neeb, John	671	D	C: 594-595	J: 356-357, 393-394; K: 89, 104-105, 113-116
Needham, Edgar H.	300	D	B: 609-810	F: 606, 624; G: 9, 17, 502, 511, 512-514
Needham, Jessie Ruby	300	M	G: 94	G: 502, 514-515
Neil/Niel, Sarah C.	124	M	A: 137	D: 225
Nelson, Perry	90	D	A: 102	D: 35, 40, 234, 239, 248, 251-253
Newsome, Amos	799	D	D: 35	L: 58, 72-73, 124, 130-131, 236, 290, 320, 326-327, 334-338, 504-505
Newton, Henry S.	67	D	A: 78	B: 251, 265, 266, 281
Nichols/Nickols, Harry W.	309	D	B: 633-634	F: 651, 656, 671, 681-682
Nolf, Peter	815	D	D: 53	L: 167-168, 204-205, 206, 209-210; M: 152-153, 181-184
Northcutt, Madison	284	D	B: 573-574	F: 514, 515, 526, 547, 557, 629, 752, 763
Northup, Charles H.	441	D	C: 72-73	H: 34, 57-58, 59, 69, 70-71
Nunn, Hugh	917	D	D: 157	M: 450
Nurenberg, M.	468	D	C: 134-135	H: 223, 231-232, 248
Nutting, Hiram	68	D	A: 81	C: 9-10; D: 28-29, 31-32
O'Gorman, Thomas	662	D	C: 570-571, 604-605, 705	J: 263, 309-310
O'Grady, Mary	901	D	D: 141	M: 271, 301, 335-336, 346; N: 263-264, 273-274, 283-285, 286-289
O'Keefe, David	574	D	C: 378-379	I: 305-306, 347-348
O'Leary, Patrick	826	I	D: 64	L: 277-278, 288-290, 303; M: 228-229, 241, 268-269

Name	File #	Type	Fee Book & Register	Minute Book
O'Moore, George (also Moore, George O.)	543	D	C: 302-303	I: 79-80, 114-115, 585-586; J: 159-161, 223; M: 169, 192, 193-194, 430-431, 461-463
Offutt, Charles	1025	D	D: 272	O: 344, 378, 389-390, 527
Ogan, David P. V.	548	D	C: 316-317	I: 167, 184, 192-193, 255; J: 59, 86-88, 93, 158, 165, 167-171, 173-174
Ogan, David P. V.	650	M	C: 544-545	J: 185, 582-583; K: 398; N: 530-531, 568, 605-606; O: 25, 45-48, 283-284, 300, 302-303
Ogan, Kittie/Kitty V.	649	M	C: 542-543	J: 186, 582, 583; K: 397; N: 530-531, 568, 605-606; O: 25, 45-48, 283-284, 300, 302-303
Ogan, Mary A.	648	M	C: 540-541	J: 186, 582-583; K: 398; N: 530-531, 568, 605-606; O: 25, 45-48, 283-284, 300, 302-303
Ordway, Drucilla Helen	333	M		G: 186-187, 191, 206, 236, 244-246
Ordway, Martha Jane	333	M		G: 186-187, 191, 206, 236, 244-246
Ordway, Mary Abby	333	M		G: 186-187, 191, 206, 236, 244-246
Ordway, William	333	D	B: 695-696; C: 476-477	G: 39, 44-45, 291, 323, 326; H: 281; I: 111, 141-143, 584; J: 9-10, 20, 98-101, 129-130, 139-140, 150-153, 188-189, 212-213, 235-236, 237-240, 252
Orr, Mary Ann	1056	D	D: 303	O: 526-527
Osborn/Osburn, William	357	D	B: 749-750	G: 114, 123-124, 144, 159, 559, 567, 576-577, 578
Ottman, Mary	689	D	C: 636-637	J: 480-481, 492-493, 506; K: 2, 3, 51-54, 406; L: 63-64, 66-67, 75, 77-78, 293, 319, 352-353
Overton, John W.	768	D	D: 4	K: 333, 370-371, 382; L: 312-313, 349-351
Owen, Thomas H.	980	I	D: 225	N: 602-603, 611-612, 635; O: 71-72, 113, 123-125, 330, 342-343
Owens, John B.	373	D	B: 783-784	G: 397, 405, 491-493
Paine, Clara E.	515	M	C: 236-237	H: 538
Paine, Etta/Ettie K.	515	M	C: 236-237	H: 538
Paine, Lula	515	M	C: 236-237	H: 538
Palmer, Lottie Bertha	391	M	B: 819-820	G: 286, 295-296
Pangburn, Annie Eugenia	748	M	C: 762-763	K: 218-219

Name	File #	Type	Fee Book & Register	Minute Book
Patterson, Rebecca	412	D	C: 14-15	G: 458, 481, 486, 487, 501; H: 169-170, 182, 195-196, 209, 218, 409
Patterson, William H.	346	D	B: 725-726	G: 92
Patton, Robert A.	182	M	B: 177-178	E: 281, 297, 307
Pauli, Heloisa S.	572	I	C: 374-375	I: 284, 290, 296-297, 348-351, 379-381
Payne, Hannah	819	M	D: 57	L: 213, 220-221
Payne, Newton	819	M	D: 57	L: 213, 220-221
Pennypacker, Mary	69	D	A: 82	B: 114, 116, 131, 160-161, 182, 195-196, 206, 242, 262-263
Peter, John	72	D	A: 83; B: 477-478	B: 219-220, 243, 258, 261-262, 264, 372; F: 273, 291-292, 575, 586
Peterson, Ann Frances	365	M	B: 767-768	G: 170
Peterson, Dick	365	M	B: 767-768	G: 170
Peterson, Jane Ellen	365	M	B: 767-768	G: 170
Peterson, Nathaniel Houston	365	M	B: 767-768	G: 170
Phillips, John	485	I	C: 168-169	H: 308, 310
Philpot, Marion Jariat	188	M	B: 219-220	E: 329, 330, 357, 370; F: 787; G: 6-7, 9, 398; H: 211, 265, 284; K: 99-100
Philpot, William Addison	188	M	B: 219-220	E: 329, 330, 357, 370; F: 787; G: 6-7, 9, 398; H: 211, 265, 284; K: 99-100
Phinney, Roswell	788	D	D: 24	L: 5, 22, 43-44, 46, 110-111, 117-118, 119-120, 412, 626; M: 51-56, 161-162, 176, 194, 197, 219-221, 233, 369, 401, 414
Pickett, James	600	D	C: 440-441	I: 505, 521-522; J: 116-117
Pierce, Arthur L.	399	M		G: 572-573, 584
Pierce, Lewis/Louis A.	744	D	C: 750-751	K: 172, 183-184, 189, 202, 214-216, 224-225, 238, 281-284, 338, 361-363; L: 36-37, 50-51, 206, 232, 248-249, 286-287
Pierce, Solomon	399	D	B: 833-834	G: 330, 337, 342, 573, 584; H: 206, 210, 231, 241, 265, 273, 279
Pierce, William S.	604	M	C: 448-449	I: 525-526, 554-555
Piña, Antonio	71	D	A: 70	B: 106, 178-179
Piña, German	70	D	A: 82	B: 76, 106, 179
Piña, Lazaro	16	D	A: 17	
Piña, Maria Antonia	216	M	B: 343-344	E: 556; F: 388

Name	File #	Type	Fee Book & Register	Minute Book
Plank, Jacob Heber	737	D	C: 736-737	K: 130, 140-141, 142, 216, 347-351
Pollok/Pollock, E. E. (Mrs.)	857	D	D: 96	L: 565, 594-596
Pomeroy, Walter	150	D	B: 17-18, 193-194, 423-424, 427-428	E: 39, 44, 53-54, 122, 138, 157, 304, 452; F: 124, 127, 134, 135, 137, 152, 184, 197
Pond, Mary	368	M	B: 773-774, 783-784	G: 195, 202, 214, 225, 239, 262-264, 471, 495, 516-517
Pool/Poole, George W.	507	D	C: 216-217	H: 503, 509, 528; I: 388, 407-411
Pool/Poole, Kenney/Kinney	560	D	C: 348-349	I: 182, 333-334, 465, 484, 503, 559; J: 3-5, 48, 53-55, 453, 476-477
Pope, William	1	D	A: 1	
Poppe, J. A.	1051	D	D: 298	O: 509, 528-529
Post, J. H.	988	D	D: 233	O: 26, 62, 107
Pots/Potts, Martha A.	123	M	A: 137	D: 226-227
Powers, Edward	6	D	A: 7	
Prewett, Francis Graham	238	M	B: 491-492	F: 303, 305-306, 329, 340, 372, 388, 391; I: 359, 370, 391, 392, 524-525, 543-544
Prewett, Francis Graham	607	M	C: 454-455	I: 547-548, 558; J: 337-338
Prewett, George	238	M	B: 491-492	F: 303, 305-306, 329, 340, 372, 388, 391; I: 360, 370, 392, 393-394, 525, 544-546
Prewett, George	607	M	C: 454-455	I: 547-548, 558; J: 337-338
Prewett, John	238	D	B: 445-446, 491-492, 529-530	F: 208, 222-223, 242, 249, 255, 283-284, 288, 297, 303, 308, 367-368, 372, 385, 412, 481, 508-511, 553, 558, 674, 675, 690-693, 700
Prewett, Martha Ann	238	M	B: 491-492	F: 303, 305-306, 329, 340, 372, 388, 391; I: 359-360, 370, 392-393
Price, Henry Lucas	126	M	A: 138	D: 237; I: 558, 574
Price, Pitman Hardin	126	M	A: 138	D: 237; I: 558, 574, 589-591
Prudon, Victor	417	D	C: 22-23	G: 483, 485-486, 497, 518, 532, 545, 551-553; H: 63, 65, 80, 87
Puckett, G. W.	487	I	C: 172-173	H: 309, 320, 321-322, 338, 348, 353-354
Pugh, Benjamin C.	349	D	B: 733-734	G: 95, 103, 106, 124, 127, 138, 142, 275, 293, 297-298, 307, 323, 332-333
Pugh, Melvina	262	M	B: 519-520	F: 360

Name	File #	Type	Fee Book & Register	Minute Book
Purvine, Charles	424	D	C: 36-37, 556-557	G: 528, 540, 541, 641-642; H: 179, 421, 455-457, 458, 472, 486-487, 550, 596; J: 187, 242-243, 251, 280-284
Purvine, Charles Francis	505	M	C: 208-209	H: 457, 473, 485-486
Purvine, Margaret Josephine	505	M	C: 208-209	H: 457, 473, 485-486
Purvine, Thomas Byron	505	M	C: 208-209	H: 457, 473, 485-486
Purvine, Walter S.	505	M	C: 208-209	H: 457, 473, 485-486
Purvine, William	505	M	C: 208-209	H: 457, 473, 485-486
Pyatt, Cornelia	992	D	D: 237	O: 75, 76, 120, 125-126, 134
Pyatt, Thomas H.	479	D	C: 158-159	H: 290, 299, 304, 368; I: 465-466; J: 112; K: 413, 427-428; M: 594, 614
Rackliff, Edgar	633	M	C: 510-511	J: 111
Rackliff, Ella	633	M	C: 510-511	J: 111
Rackliff, Eugene	633	M	C: 510-511	J: 111
Rackliff, P. K.	547	D	C: 314-315	I: 148, 164-165, 169, 187-188, 205-206, 336-337; J: 28, 50, 65-69
Rackliff, Willie	633	M	C: 510-511	J: 111
Ragan, Weldon H.	773	D	D: 9	K: 373-374, 382-383
Ragsdale, Thomas N.	1050	D	D: 297	O: 497, 518, 522
Rambo, Ann	550	D	C: 320-321	I: 147, 177-178; J: 497, 508-511
Rambo, Isaac	184	D	B: 185-186	E: 294, 300, 309, 325, 336, 385, 538, 539-540
Rambo, Milton	335	D	B: 699-700	G: 14, 22-23
Rand, Joseph	558	D	C: 344-345	I: 183-184, 241-242, 256; J: 175, 203-204
Rand, Oliver	386	D	B: 807-808; C: 222-223	G: 274, 282, 286, 287, 292, 649, 655; H: 162, 181-182, 190, 199, 204, 234-235, 512, 528
Raney, Helen A.	877	D	D: 116	M: 72, 90-91, 92, 163-164, 421-422, 434-438, 611, 638-640; N: 1, 79-80, 106-109, 174-175
Raney, John B.	577	D	C: 386-387	I: 335, 365-366, 371-374; J: 305, 322
Ray, Benjamin M.	952	D	D: 196	N: 250-251, 265-267, 272, 562, 579-580, 590, 610, 619, 627-629
Raymond, Frank	273	D	B: 549-550, 637-638	F: 446, 451, 452, 458, 540-541, 663, 664, 665, 679-681, 711, 715-716; G: 15-16, 23-27, 50

Name	File #	Type	Fee Book & Register	Minute Book
Raymond, James M.	896	D	D: 136	M: 225, 249-250, 265, 296, 330-331, 356, 375-376, 478; N: 18, 42-43, 533-535, 555; O: 68, 92-94, 214, 232, 247-249, 250
Raymond, Mary Ann	882	D	D: 121	M: 346-347, 356, 374-375
Read, Mary Fidelia	1043	D	D: 290	O: 466-467, 490, 493
Reed, Charles H.	426	M	C: 40-42	G: 538, 628; I: 326
Reed, Emeline J.	426	M	C: 40-42	G: 538, 628; I: 326
Reed, George H.	389	D	B: 815-816	G: 281, 289-290, 291, 345, 361-362, 459, 470-471, 525, 597, 603-604
Reed, James F.	97	D	A: 110; B: 111-112	D: 68, 81, 85, 117, 350, 351, 359, 363, 367; E: 200, 217; F: 585, 602, 604, 618
Reed, James F.	679	D	C: 616-617	J: 417, 447-448, 453, 480, 498, 526; K: 150-151, 236, 271-273, 280-281, 292-293; M: 17-18, 36
Reeger, Frederic	15	D	A: 16	
Reichardt, Emma	299	M		
Reichardt, Oswald	299	D	B: 607-608	F: 601-602, 613, 614-615, 764-765
Reilly/Riley, Edward	297	D	B: 603-604	F: 583, 591-592, 601, 603, 761, 782-783; G: 29, 31, 45-46, 178, 180, 201
Rice, Alexander	181	D	B: 173-174	E: 277
Rich, John P.	236	D	B: 441-442	F: 199, 211, 232, 247
Richards, Frank	1016	M	D: 263	O: 246-247
Richards, John	1012	D	D: 259	O: 211, 224-225, 226, 261, 310-311, 314, 317-318, 336-338, 347-348, 378, 382, 400-402
Richards, William E.	622	D	C: 488-489	J: 41-42, 69-71, 97
Rien, John William	640	D	C: 524-525, 756-757	J: 159, 179, 180-181, 189, 253-254, 313-314, 348, 479, 496, 513-515, 517, 548-551; K: 95, 106-108, 168-169, 190, 209-210, 232; L: 632; M: 29-31; N: 567, 587, 619, 633; O: 49-50
Rines, Walter B.	647	D	C: 538-539	J: 177, 209-210, 254, 271, 320-321, 397-398, 561-562, 569-570, 592; K: 51, 77-80, 81
Ringstrom, Adolph	192	D	B: 231-232	E: 362, 367, 375, 384, 552-553, 560-562

Name	File #	Type	Fee Book & Register	Minute Book
Roberts, Hardin	739	D	C: 740-741	K: 144, 146, 166, 167-168, 325, 326-328
Robertson, William R.	324	D	B: 671-672, 755-756	F: 762, 775; G: 40-41, 176-177, 184; K: 262-263
Robinson, David C.	700	D	C: 658-659, 668	J: 520, 526-527, 546, 547, 554, 568, 573-574, 579-580, 619; L: 178-179, 202-203, 218-219; O: 394, 454, 484-485, 486
Rock, George	14	D	A: 15	
Rodgers, Alexander W.	629	D	C: 502-503	J: 79-80, 91-92, 104; L: 415, 435, 458-462
Rodgers/Rogers, John	319	D	B: 663-664	F: 747, 757; G: 38-39, 87-88, 151, 346, 365, 398; H: 128
Rogers, Lewis G.	733	D	C: 728-729	K: 119, 136-137, 200-201, 227-232
Rolett/Rowlett, Henry	293	M	B: 593-594	F: 564, 571, 763, 780, 783; G: 522, 529
Rood, William W.	221	D	B: 367-368, 401-402	E: 601, 615, 632; F: 2, 35, 43, 44, 70, 84-85, 216, 240, 247, 265, 529, 538, 547
Rosaas, Tellef Christianson	753	D	C: 772-773	K: 236, 253-254, 255; L: 366-367, 379-380
Ross, Jesse	719	D	C: 700-701	J: 637; K: 13, 14-15, 49-50, 105-106, 130, 138-139, 170, 177-178, 192, 243-244
Ross, William	680	D	C: 618-619, 758-759	J: 418, 460, 464-465, 505-506; K: 27
Rowland, James	816	D	D: 54	L: 176, 185-187, 229, 246-247; M: 314-315, 385-390
Rowlett, P. H.	20	D	A: 21	
Rule, Charles Stone	570	M	C: 370-371	I: 270-271
Rule, Edward James	570	M	C: 370-371	I: 270-271
Rule, Nannie Augusta	570	M	C: 370-371	I: 270-271
Rule, William Johnston	570	M	C: 370-371	I: 270-271
Rulison, E. C. (Mrs.)	450	D	C: 94-95	H: 90, 97-98, 118, 134, 375, 390-391, 403-406, 451
Rulison, Joseph E.	446	D	C: 86-87	H: 77, 88-89, 90, 376, 394-395, 406-407

Name	File #	Type	Fee Book & Register	Minute Book
Runyon, Armistead	834	D	D: 72, 123, 180	L: 378, 405, 406-409, 434-435, 453, 455, 468-469, 499, 500-501, 503-504, 513-514, 524, 525-527; M: 2, 37-38, 100-101, 121, 129, 130, 157-158, 188, 189-192, 199-200, 202-203, 213-214, 394, 470, 506, 540-543, 548-549, 613; N: 12-14, 70-72, 103, 172, 180-181, 182, 224, 278-283, 351-359, 479-482; O: 170, 186, 196-197, 233-234, 245-246, 265-266, 385, 409, 414-417
Runyon, Charles E.	889	M	D: 129	M: 188-189, 209-210; O: 77
Runyon, Emma	889	M	D: 129	M: 188-189, 210-211
Runyon, Frederick M.	889	M	D: 129	M: 188-189, 209-210
Russell, Mary Augusta	571	M	C: 372-373	I: 275-276, 306-307, 355
Russell, Sylvester	533	D	C: 278-279	I: 14, 17-18, 59, 68, 78, 95-96, 180, 208-209, 221, 329-330
Russell, William Francis	571	M	C: 372-373	I: 275-276, 306-307, 355
Rust, Horace	497	D	C: 192-193	H: 377, 392-393, 417-418; I: 202, 222-224
Rutherford, James	855	D	D: 94	L: 538, 584, 591-592, 593; M: 41, 605; N: 17, 60-61, 585-586
Ryan, Mortimer	486	D	C: 170-171, 304-305, 548-549	H: 311, 323-324, 325, 342-345; I: 98-99, 160-161, 164, 169, 227-232, 249, 268, 291-292, 303, 313-317, 327-328, 382-383; J: 173, 198-199; K: 315
Ryan, Pierce	270	I	B: 543-544, 657-658; C: 148-149	F: 439, 450, 459-460, 522, 527, 688, 689, 694, 704, 714, 718, 719, 725, 734-738; G: 257; H: 211, 220, 235, 263, 273, 276, 397, 512, 571-572
Sacry, James W.	322	D	B: 669-670; C: 604-605	F: 746, 750, 751, 790, 793; G: 10, 12, 125, 134, 139, 242, 259-261, 654; J: 386, 401
Sallee, Emma		M		G: 223
Salmon, Sidney	718	D	C: 698-699	J: 632; K: 68-69, 70; M: 565, 591-592
Salter, A. C.	397	D	B: 829-830	G: 327, 331, 357, 373, 388, 389, 583, 602, 603, 605, 612, 615, 634-636
Sampson, Frederick	96	D	A: 109	D: 67, 80, 114, 119, 271
Sandford, Louis N.	557	M	C: 342-343	I: 191, 192; K: 75-76

Name	File #	Type	Fee Book & Register	Minute Book
Sansbury, William Hamilton	251	D	B: 485-486	F: 287, 296, 311, 321, 419, 644, 653
Sartor, Antonio	943	D	D: 187	N: 178-179, 237-239, 295; O: 31-32
Schartze, John	7	D	A: 8	
Schults, Martha A.	764	D	C: 798-799	K: 309-310, 334-335, 344, 358
Sciapacasa, Antonio	493	D	C: 184-185	H: 366, 401-402, 422; I: 549, 550; J: 51, 124-125, 157, 158, 196-198, 247, 255, 272-274, 494-495
Scott, Anna Maria	757	M	C: 782-785; D: 183	K: 308; M: 168, 586-587, 616-617, 618; O: 282, 296-297
Scott, Luke	887	M	D: 127	M: 149-150, 153-155, 156, 161, 244-245, 301-303; N: 18, 58-60, 207-208; O: 472
Scott, Mary W.	5	M	A: 5-6	
Scott, Thomas	757	D	C: 782-785; D: 183	K: 264-265, 306-307, 392, 418; L: 209, 222, 359, 371, 374, 432, 458, 464-465, 571; M: 36, 211, 229-230, 272-273, 274; O: 281-282, 285-287
Scott, Thomas	777	D	D: 13	K: 400, 412, 414, 422, 425-426; L: 13-14, 59-61, 421-422, 423, 448-452, 496; M: 559-560, 622; N: 8-9, 127, 138-140, 182-183, 217-219
Scott, W. T.	909	D	D: 149	M: 428, 562, 573-575, 624; N: 15-17, 125, 136-137
Scott, William W.	5	D	A: 5	
Sears, William James	977	D	D: 222	N: 597, 616-617, 634; O: 21, 103, 115, 128-130
Seawell, Thomas H.	224	D	B: 389-390, 509-510	F: 54, 57, 66, 250, 289-290, 316, 330, 366-367
Segrat, Christopher	318	D	B: 661-662	F: 739, 743, 748-749
Seilor, Peter	80	D	A: 93	B: 310-311, 311BB, 315, 319; D: 163, 187
Sharon, Adelaide L.	540	M	C: 296-297	I: 70, 88
Sharon, Edmund M.	540	M	C: 296-297	I: 70, 88
Sharon, John	443	D	C: 76-77	H: 55, 62, 76, 454, 474-476, 488; L: 3, 56-57
Sharon, Margaretta R.	540	M	C: 296-297	I: 70, 88
Shattuck, Gilbert	614	D	C: 468-469	I: 593; J: 16, 32, 34, 56, 82-85, 102-103, 117-119; L: 21-22, 38, 39-41
Shaw, Charles B.	996	M	D: 241	O: 88, 120, 133

Name	File #	Type	Fee Book & Register	Minute Book
Shaw, Ella L.	996	M	D: 241	O: 88, 120, 133
Shaw, Louisa T.	959	D	D: 203	N: 349-350, 371-372, 373, 531-532; O: 87, 117-118, 161
Shaw, Mary Francis	337	D	B: 701-702	G: 17, 34, 70, 81, 94, 100, 103, 146
Shearer, Henry	77	D	A: 90	B: 83-84, 85-86, 97, 106, 109, 166, 169-171
Shelford, John	878	D	D: 117	M: 99-100, 122-123, 124, 233-234; N: 604-605, 625-627; O: 7, 15-19
Sheridan, Flan	760	D	C: 788-789	K: 285-286, 297-299, 355-356; L: 383, 388-393
Shinn, Andrew Jackson	345	M		G: 229, 238; K: 146-147, 156-158
Shinn, Andrew Jackson	743	M	C: 748-749	K: 161-162, 222, 250-252, 379-380, 393, 394-395
Shinn, Eliza Jane	345	M		G: 229, 238; K: 146-147, 156-158
Shinn, Eliza Jane	743	M	C: 748-749	K: 161-162, 222, 250-252, 379-380, 393, 394-395
Shinn, Ellen	345	M		G: 229, 238; K: 146-147, 156-158
Shinn, John Davis	345	M		G: 229, 238; K: 146-147, 156-158
Shinn, John Davis	743	M	C: 748-749	K: 161-162, 222, 250-252, 379-380, 393, 394-395
Shinn, John O.	345	D	B: 721-722	G: 91, 100-101, 117, 239, 258; K: 117-118
Shinn, Mary Ellen	743	M	C: 748-749	K: 161-162, 222, 250-252, 379-380, 393, 394-395
Shinn, Robert F.	345	M		G: 229, 238; K: 146-147, 156-158
Shinn, Sisalone	345	M		G: 229, 238; K: 146-147, 156-158
Shuler, John M.	694	D	C: 646-647	J: 493-494, 502-503, 525
Sime, C. S.	403	D	B: 841-842	G: 366-367, 372-373, 648-649, 655; H: 22, 44, 50-51, 84, 103, 108-109, 118, 128, 134-135
Simmons, Charles	597	M	C: 434-435	I: 500
Simmons, Dulana	962	D	D: 206	N: 406-407, 451-452, 478-479, 557, 575-576, 603-604; O: 108, 116, 320, 329, 340, 351, 356-357, 364-365, 390-392
Simmons, Ida	597	M	C: 434-435	I: 500
Simmons, James S.	976	M	D: 221	N: 556, 558-559, 581-582; O: 452
Simmons, Monroe	598	D	C: 436-437	I: 500, 510-511
Simpson, Amanda M.	849	D	D: 88	L: 509, 533-535; N: 205-206, 243-244, 245-248

Name	File #	Type	Fee Book & Register	Minute Book
Simpson, Ernest Alroy	368	M	B: 773-774, 783-784	G: 195, 202, 214, 225, 239, 262-264, 376-377, 471, 495, 516-517, 582; H: 490, 494-495; L: 6, 47-49; O: 10-11, 39, 195-196, 322-324
Simpson, R. Michael	368	M	B: 773-774, 783-784	G: 195, 202, 214, 225, 239, 262-264, 376-377, 471, 495, 516-517, 582; H: 490, 494-495; L: 6, 47-49; O: 10-11, 39, 195-196, 322-324
Sipe, Charles H.	415	M	C: 18-19	G: 519
Skaggs, Elijah	190	D	B: 225-226, 283-284	E: 346, 360-361, 367, 368, 434, 585; G: 534-535
Skaggs, Emma L.	190	M	B: 599-600	F: 573, 578, 581; H: 411; I: 256-257; K: 211; M: 596-597; O: 291
Slattery, Michael	275	D	B: 553-554	F: 452, 464, 465, 529; I: 202, 221, 239
Smith, Abbie	724	M	C: 710-711	K: 23
Smith, Adaline D.	416	M	C: 20-21	G: 480, 602
Smith, Albert O.	416	M	C: 20-21	G: 480, 602
Smith, Chauncey B.	416	M	C: 20-21	G: 480, 602
Smith, D. S.	139	D	A: 153	B: 157
Smith, Elanor/Elenora	137	M	A: 151	D: 178
Smith, Eliza	85	M	A: 97-98, 163	B: 93-94, 99-100
Smith, Ezekiel	137	M	A: 151	D: 178
Smith, George	78	D	A: 91	B: 55-56, 81, 94, 119, 135, 137, 142-144, 155-156, 188, 194, 205, 214-215, 241, 286, 292, 304-305, 376
Smith, George	989	I	D: 234	O: 22, 54, 73
Smith, George Taylor	634	M	C: 512-513	J: 112, 114-115, 241, 245-246, 391-392
Smith, George W.	98	M	A: 111; B: 41-42, 107-108	D: 83, 128, 151, 153, 154, 205-206; E: 59, 156
Smith, Giles	315	D	B: 653-654	F: 701, 708, 709, 740-742; H: 163
Smith, Governeur	304	M		G: 59-60
Smith, Harry	932	M	D: 172	M: 412-413
Smith, Henry	304	D	B: 619-620	F: 619, 628, 636, 643, 662; G: 53, 56-59

Name	File #	Type	Fee Book & Register	Minute Book
Smith, Hiram	85	D	A: 97-98, 163; B: 9-10, 705-706	B: 65-66, 67-71, 73-75, 105, 172-173, 174, 179-180, 186, 343-344, 366, 367; D: 43, 52, 83, 322, 331, 341, 361; E: 15, 38, 40, 153, 164, 261, 274-275; G: 42-43, 51, 97-99
Smith, Isaac B.	98	M	A: 111; B: 41-42, 107-108	D: 83, 128, 151, 153, 154, 205-206; E: 59, 156
Smith, Isaac Parsons	1011	D	D: 258	O: 195, 231-232, 277-278, 300, 328
Smith, Jacob	661	D	C: 568-569	J: 250-251, 252-253, 270-271, 294, 341-342, 638; K: 15, 17-18, 31-34; L: 8, 62, 79, 92, 98-102; M: 44
Smith, James B.	137	M	A: 151	D: 178
Smith, James B.	159	M	B: 183-184, 253-254, 361-362, 435-436, 635-636; C: 12-13	E: 76, 103, 255, 378, 382, 394-395, 408, 490, 497, 499-505, 513, 555, 581-582, 587-588, 589-593, 612, 616-617, 618, 626-629; F: 38, 44-53, 105, 156, 174-175, 251, 253, 258-261, 262, 335-336, 338-339, 362, 376, 377-383, 410, 418, 480, 484, 485-491, 535, 600-601, 606-612, 655, 762, 766-771; G: 83, 108-109, 110-112, 174-175, 309, 314-318, 319, 439, 445-451; H: 230, 241-244; I: 227, 251-254, 564-565; J: 603
Smith, James M.	85	M	A: 97-98, 163	D: 62, 69
Smith, Jerome B.	848	D	D: 87	L: 507, 543, 567-569; M: 38, 362-363, 396, 633
Smith, John	756	D	C: 780-781	K: 258, 269-270, 378; L: 159, 183, 185, 192-193; M: 508
Smith, John Henry	416	M	C: 20-21	G: 480, 602
Smith, John P.	85	M	A: 97-98, 163; B: 39-40	B: 173, 345, 349-350, 351-352, 364, 376, 424, 427; C: 5; D: 358; E: 26, 32, 57, 68-69, 91, 92, 94-98, 109-110, 126, 131
Smith, Manuela	159	M	B: 63-64, 251-252, 359-360, 433-434	E: 76, 103, 255, 377, 382, 389-391, 408, 490, 497, 499-505, 513, 555, 581-584, 589-593, 612, 616-617, 618, 626-629; F: 38, 44-53, 105, 156, 169-171, 251, 253, 258-261, 262, 336-339
Smith, Martha J.	137	M	A: 151	D: 178

Name	File #	Type	Fee Book & Register	Minute Book
Smith, Napoleon B.	98	M	A: 111; B: 41-42	D: 83, 128, 151, 153, 154, 205-206; E: 59, 250, 255
Smith, Preston B.	656	D	C: 558-559	J: 245, 268, 269-270, 279, 286-287, 326-329, 367-369
Smith, Robert E.	246	D	B: 467-468, 591-592	F: 233, 254, 271, 285, 309, 344, 356, 364, 402, 477, 506, 533-534, 539, 551-552, 619, 626, 638, 643, 648
Smith, S. S.	827	D	D: 65	L: 292, 309, 317-318, 510, 585-589; M: 106, 132-133, 304, 317-321, 551
Smith, Sarah C.	672	M	C: 596-597	J: 360
Smith, Soloman	138	D	A: 152	B: 84-85, 96, 97, 98, 103-104, 118, 136-137, 164, 167, 168-169
Smith, Stephen (Capt.)	74	D	A: 85-88; B: 29-30, 101-102	B: 187, 188-189, 192-193, 206, 207-209, 215-216, 225-234, 259-260, 282, 283, 301, 362-363, 372, 375, 386, 419, 420, 424; C: 4; D: 25, 86, 106-107, 140-142, 143-144, 238, 249, 255, 259, 269, 278; E: 5, 47, 66, 73-76, 77, 100, 103, 111, 119, 126, 141, 153, 156, 165, 219, 228-232
Smith, Stephen M.	159	M	B: 65-66, 255-256, 363-364, 437-438	E: 76, 103, 254, 377, 383, 392-393, 409, 490, 497, 499-505, 513, 555, 581-582, 584-586, 589-593, 612, 616-617, 618, 626-629; F: 38, 44-53, 105, 157, 171-173, 251, 253, 258-261, 262, 334-335, 338-339, 362, 376, 377-383, 410, 418
Smith/Smyth, Ann T.	286	D	B: 577-578	F: 519, 528, 536, 559, 573-574, 635
Snoddy, Benjamin A.	527	D	C: 262-263	H: 573; I: 10-11, 17, 171-172, 220-221; J: 201, 214, 228-230; K: 12
Snyder, Jacob R.	956	D	D: 200	N: 298-299, 335-337, 359-360, 367-369, 370-371, 380-382, 389-391, 476-477, 498; O: 492-493, 515
Snyder/Snider, Charles C.	227	D	B: 395-396, 425-426	F: 62, 79, 97, 136, 143-144, 153, 161-162, 181, 192, 220, 304, 321-324, 448
Snyder/Snider, Ella	227	M	B: 517-518	F: 363-364, 375, 376, 398-399, 430, 468

Name	File #	Type	Fee Book & Register	Minute Book
Southard, Platt	86	D	A: 98	B: 222-223, 243, 244-245, 253, 266-267, 294, 298-299, 383, 386, 392, 396, 405-406
Speers, William B.	859	D	D: 98, 181	L: 577, 607, 608-609, 614, 634-635; M: 13, 33-34, 73-74, 200-201, 341, 358-359, 466, 514-515, 532, 533, 570-571, 572, 575-576, 592-593; N: 45, 140-141, 200-201, 551-552, 560, 576-577, 585, 599, 618, 632; O: 7, 33-35
Spence, George	79	D	A: 92	B: 140, 147-148, 316-317
Spence, John F.	260	D	B: 507-508	F: 353, 366, 396, 427, 569, 577
Spencer, Charles	897	M	D: 137	M: 250-251
Spencer, George	897	M	D: 137	M: 250-251
Spencer, Nancy	897	M	D: 137	M: 250-251
Spencer, Rowena	897	M	D: 137	M: 250-251
Spencer, Shattuck	897	M	D: 137	M: 250-251
Sprague, Elijah/Elisha	404	D	B: 843-844	G: 367, 374, 388, 397, 401, 475, 631, 650; H: 4, 8-9, 25, 208
Spriggs, Thomas	73	D	A: 84; B: 7-8, 215-216, 285-286, 309-310; C: 6-7	B: 75, 178, 200-201, 212-213, 250-251, 254-255, 286, 296-297, 318; D: 359, 379; E: 3, 6, 8, 9, 18, 217-218, 223, 234, 243, 246, 252, 258, 259, 265, 267, 268, 273, 285, 315, 320-321, 326, 356, 371, 375, 384-385, 399, 400, 435-437, 461, 474-478, 508-509, 518, 537, 562-569; F: 158-159; G: 264-265, 301, 304, 306, 307, 327, 330, 375, 386, 420-423
Springer, James Lemont	1026	D	D: 273	O: 366, 381, 419-421
Sproule, George W.	808	M	D: 46	L: 138, 142, 168-169, 213-214, 231-232
Squires, Harvey/Henry	264	I	B: 525-526	F: 393, 403, 404, 415, 428, 433-434, 463, 470-471; G: 366, 371
St. Clair, David	92	D	A: 105	B: 175, 176, 311, 310AA, 312, 318, 328, 336-340, 364, 375, 379-380, 384, 394; D: 37, 45, 73, 74-75
St. Clair, Francis Marion	198	M	B: 261-262	D: 37; E: 421, 422
St. Clair, William Wallace	198	M	B: 261-262	D: 37; E: 421, 422
St. John, A. C.	825	D	D: 63	L: 276-277, 310-311, 369-370; M: 1, 428, 448-449

Name	File #	Type	Fee Book & Register	Minute Book
Stab, Clement	463	D	C: 122-123	H: 184, 196-198, 239-240, 340-341; I: 4, 23-25, 274-275, 342-345, 346-347
Staley, Frederick	692	D	C: 642-643	J: 484, 500, 507, 521, 540-541, 563
Stanley, Ann C.	803	D	D: 39	L: 89, 114-115, 137, 373, 428, 429, 430-431; M: 170-171, 194-196, 294, 321-322, 429-430, 432, 464-466, 587, 602-604; O: 448-449
Stark, William	211	D	B: 323-324	E: 522, 523, 534; F: 58, 91, 110
Starr, Winfield	336	M	B: 699-700; C: 212-213	G: 192; H: 264, 281, 282-284, 417, 443-445, 454, 484-485; J: 527, 535-536; K: 379
Steadman, Amos D.	960	D	D: 204	N: 377, 394-395, 396, 453-454, 515-516, 540-541; O: 69, 70, 147, 510, 530-533
Steadman, Ida M.	655	M	C: 554-555	J: 246
Steele, Jehu	531	D	C: 274-275	I: 9, 27-28, 525, 550-551, 552-553
Steele, Julius A.	852	D	D: 91	L: 529, 548-549, 566, 575-576; M: 196-197
Stephens, A. L.	905	D	D: 145	M: 364, 399-400, 423, 471, 477-478, 503, 511-512, 535-537; N: 621, 630; O: 6, 19, 24, 436, 463-465
Stephens, William H.	272	M	B: 547-548	F: 455, 458
Sterling, Charles B.	75	D	A: 89	B: 88, 89, 96, 106, 108, 160, 168, 176-177, 183, 187
Sterling, Elizabeth	76	M	A: 89; B: 3-4, 375-376	B: 161, 371-372; D: 44, 56, 92, 109, 124, 157; E: 26, 36-37, 55, 180, 190, 200, 266; F: 11, 27, 432, 436-437, 620, 631, 636, 637, 639; G: 11, 16, 18-19; H: 261, 267-268, 288
Stevens, William A.	202	D	B: 289-290, 369-370	E: 444-445, 447, 453-454, 488, 494; F: 201, 224-225, 237, 247-248, 384, 391-392
Stevenson, James S.	581	D	C: 396-397	I: 390, 411-412
Stewart, Abel	226	D	B: 393-394, 409-410	F: 63-64, 81, 82, 193, 416, 425, 435, 448, 472, 712; G: 2-4, 295
Stewart, Frank Lester	709	M	C: 676-677	J: 599-600
Stewart, James W.	703	D	C: 664-665	J: 556-557, 574-576, 582, 600
Stewart, John	203	M		G: 269
Stewart, Nancy	203	D	B: 299-300	E: 480, 487, 488, 522; G: 257, 269

Name	File #	Type	Fee Book & Register	Minute Book
Stewart, Peter	1022	D	D: 269	O: 331-332, 349, 350, 354, 361-362, 373, 450
Stewart, Robert Henry	709	M	C: 676-677	J: 599-600
Stewart, William Allen	709	M	C: 676-677	J: 599-600
Stockwell, E. S.	350	D	B: 735-736	G: 104, 106, 126-127, 168, 395, 402, 431
Stombs, William P.	290	D	B: 585-586	F: 536-537, 548, 549, 553-554, 580, 587-588, 786, 788-790; G: 198
Stowell, Margaret R. E. A. B.	213	M	B: 327-328	E: 530; F: 100
Streeter, Allen C.	366	D	B: 769-770	G: 179, 196-197, 282, 302, 303, 592, 616-619
Stryker, James A.	568	M	C: 364-365	I: 250, 286-287
Stump, John C.	832	D	D: 70	L: 274, 286, 293, 328-329, 553-554; M: 238, 287-289
Stussy, David	323	D		
Stutz, Francis	163	D	B: 87-88	E: 130, 136, 150, 162, 170, 326, 333
Sullivan, Catherine M.	705	M	C: 668-669	J: 565-566
Sullivan, David	660	D	C: 566-567	J: 250, 257
Sullivan, Ellen F.	705	M	C: 668-669	J: 565-566
Sullivan, George E.	705	M	C: 668-669	J: 565-566
Sullivan, John P.	705	M	C: 668-669	J: 565-566
Swain, Georgia I.	724½	M	C: 710-711	K: 48-49
Swain, Mary D.	724½	M	C: 710-711	K: 48-49
Swain, Susan I.	724½	M	C: 710-711	K: 48-49
Swain, William Chown	723	D	C: 708-709	K: 50, 82-83
Swetland, Almira	583	D	C: 402-403	I: 404-405, 423-424, 511-512
Swetland, Orson	407	D	B: 849-850, 851	G: 375, 399-400
Swift, William M./W.	108	D	A: 124-125	D: 118, 131, 134, 138, 146, 198, 209-212, 241-243, 346, 365-366
Talbot, Kennedy Bowles	579	I	C: 390-391	I: 384-385, 394-395, 398-399, 522-523; L: 359
Tallman, Thomas	969	I	D: 213	N: 514, 518-519
Tammeyer, Caroline	518	D	C: 242-243, 600-601	H: 558, 580, 581; I: 48, 51-53, 197, 211, 243, 385-386, 411, 515-516; J: 231, 284, 285, 359, 360, 428-431, 566-568, 636, 640; K: 66-68
Tate, Augustin/Augustus E.	103	M	B: 147-148, 201-202	E: 216, 310

Name	File #	Type	Fee Book & Register	Minute Book
Tate, Jesse T.	103	M	B: 147-148, 195-196	E: 216, 310
Tate, John H.	103	M	B: 147-148, 203-204	E: 216, 310
Tate, Josefa F.	103	M	B: 147-148, 197-198	E: 216, 310; G: 615, 652; H: 1-4, 32-33, 264
Tate, Margaret Ann	103	M	B: 147-148, 199-200	E: 216, 310
Tate, Thomas H.	103	D	A: 118-119; B: 43-44, 145-146, 223-224	D: 100, 104, 129, 134, 148, 308, 332, 337, 372; E: 5, 7, 12, 31, 32, 60-63, 104, 121, 154, 162, 163, 192, 196, 207, 210-212, 218-219, 242, 258, 273, 298, 315, 323, 340-341
Taylor, Charles H.	313	D	B: 645-646	F: 695, 696, 706, 776, 779, 780, 784; G: 204, 205, 207, 218-220, 226
Taylor, Elenor	326	D	B: 675-676	F: 776, 779-780, 784; G: 270, 275, 283-284, 310-312, 343-344
Taylor, James A.	82	D	A: 94	B: 252-253, 263-264, 267, 287, 308-309, 322, 382, 412-413, 422-423, 425, 426, 428, 429-430; C: 1-2
Taylor, John	81	M	A: 93; B: 175-176	B: 76-77, 104, 130; E: 278, 301, 315, 407, 415
Taylor, Palestine	81	M	A: 93; B: 175-176	B: 76-77, 104, 130; E: 278, 301, 315, 407, 415
Taylor, Putnam	81	M	A: 93; B: 175-176	B: 76-77, 104, 130; E: 278, 301, 315, 407, 415
Taylor, Wayne	81	M	A: 93; B: 175-176	B: 76-77, 104; E: 407, 415
Tennent, Archibald	109	D	A: 126; B: 59-60	D: 115-116, 133, 200, 213, 214, 222; E: 3, 10, 88, 107, 123
Tennent, Isabel Eva	552	M	C: 326-327	I: 118, 150, 158-159, 184-186, 247, 297, 322-324, 325; J: 596
Terrill/Terrell, Samuel N.	84	D	A: 96	B: 421, 427, 429; C: 7-8; D: 30, 35, 77, 78, 201-202, 223, 237, 246, 253, 256
Thacker, Daniel	484	D	C: 166-167	H: 301, 334-335, 336; I: 271, 287, 304, 311
Thielemann/Thielman, Christian	243	D	B: 459-460	F: 230, 244, 263, 276, 309, 310, 422

Name	File #	Type	Fee Book & Register	Minute Book
Thielemann/Thielman, Mary	243	M	B: 459-460	G: 574, 590, 616; H: 9-12, 103, 111-113
Thielemann/Thielman, Otto	243	M	B: 459-460	G: 574, 590, 616; H: 9-12, 103, 111-113
Thistle, James M.	425	D	C: 38-39	G: 531, 539, 540, 561, 567-568; H: 12-13, 165, 240-241, 271; I: 8
Thomas, Adaline (Mrs.)	249	D	B: 475-476	F: 249, 272, 314, 374, 400-401, 450, 465-466, 518
Thomas, Charles B.	767	D	D: 3	K: 332, 354, 376, 377; O: 505-506, 522
Thomas, Edward C.	696	D	C: 650-651	J: 498, 512-513
Thompson, Christopher C.	824	D	D: 62	L: 276, 298, 299, 304, 398-399, 480-482, 546-547, 560-565, 597-598, 599-602
Thornley, Henry	207	D	B: 313-314	E: 510, 514, 526
Thurgood, Elizabeth Margaret	233	M		F: 718, 724, 739; H: 133, 148, 149, 166-168, 578-580; I: 72, 89-93, 115-116, 143-144, 183, 211, 212-213
Thurgood, Elizabeth Margaret	639	M	C: 522-523	J: 149-150; L: 456, 527, 546, 584; M: 402-403, 478-480, 567-568; N: 199, 237, 267
Thurgood, Margaret G.	632	D	C: 508-509, 694-695	J: 103, 133-134, 138, 139, 149, 212, 217-218, 241, 357-358, 417, 456, 462, 471-472, 629-630, 634; K: 9-11, 208, 411-412, 430-432; L: 37, 79, 86, 90-92, 96, 381, 401-403, 419-420, 438-440
Thurgood, Mary Ann	233	M		F: 718, 724, 739; H: 133, 148, 149, 166-168, 578-580; I: 72, 89-93, 115-116, 143-144, 183, 211, 212-213
Thurgood, Mary Ann	639	M	C: 522-523	J: 149-150; L: 456, 527, 546, 584; M: 402-403, 478-480, 567-568; N: 199, 237, 267
Thurgood, William Sharp	233	D	B: 415-416; C: 112-113	F: 104, 118-119, 595, 668, 675, 689, 697-699
Thurgood, William Sharp	233	M		F: 718, 724, 739; H: 133, 148, 149, 166-168, 578-580; I: 72, 89-93, 115-116, 143-144, 183, 211, 212-213

Name	File #	Type	Fee Book & Register	Minute Book
Thurgood, William Sharp	639	M	C: 522-523	J: 149-150; L: 456, 527, 546, 584; M: 402-403, 478-480, 567-568; N: 199, 237, 267
Timms, Anthony	305	I	B: 621-622	F: 619-620, 626-627
Tobin, Patrick	168	M	B: 115-116	E: 169, 180
Totten, Edward	130	M	A: 142	D: 266-267, 317, 330, 374-375
Totten, George Mansfield	130	M	A: 142	D: 266-267, 317, 330, 374-375
Tracy, Charles	935	M	D: 175	M: 413, 418, 463-464
Tracy, Dora	935	M	D: 175	M: 413, 418, 463-464
Tracy, Eda	935	M	D: 175	M: 413, 418, 463-464
Tracy, Phoebe	935	M	D: 175	M: 413, 418, 463-464
Travers, Theodore O.	17	M	A: 18	
Travers, William M.	17	M	A: 18	
Travis, Whitely	362	D	B: 761-762	G: 165, 174, 178
Trayon/Trahern, J. D.	13	D	A: 14	B: 59, 67, 71
Treadway, Amelia	314	D	B: 649-650	F: 703, 713, 714, 716, 722, 723; G: 19, 20
Treadway, John S.	185	D	B: 187-188, 347-348, 781-782	E: 294-295, 300, 311, 384, 456-457, 462, 575-576, 602-603; F: 39, 56, 86-87, 160, 168, 179, 190, 202, 211, 232, 241; G: 221, 222, 228, 271, 278-279, 405-406
Trimble, George	950	M	D: 194	N: 236-237, 343; O: 242, 256-257
Trimble, Louis/Lewis	950	M	D: 194	N: 236-237, 343; O: 242, 256-257
Trimble, Lucy E.	950	M	D: 194	N: 236-237, 343; O: 242, 256-257
Trimble, William Henry	835	D	D: 73	L: 385, 428, 445-446, 462, 554; M: 38-39, 410, 418, 508-509, 561, 586, 601, 612-613, 623; N: 28, 61, 105
Truitt, James H.	458	D	C: 110-111	H: 130, 143, 180; I: 71-72, 81-84
Trumbull, Luther	83	I	A: 95	B: 311BB, 323-324
Turner, Cornelius J.	176	M	B: 265-266	E: 424
Turner, Henry C.	822	D	D: 60	L: 236-237, 295-296, 371, 374-375, 445; O: 368, 396
Turner, Jasper N.	176	M	B: 267-268	E: 424
Turner, Jonas	176	D	B: 153-154, 171-172	E: 233, 243, 248, 249, 253, 265, 266, 343, 411, 418-420; F: 60-61
Turner, Serepta A.	176	M	B: 269-270	E: 424
Turney, James W.	200	D	B: 271-272, 417-418	E: 426, 429, 434, 442; F: 96, 101, 104-105, 117-118, 149-150

Name	File #	Type	Fee Book & Register	Minute Book
Tustin, Samuel	228	D	B: 397-398, 557-558	F: 67, 83, 93-94, 324, 348-349, 414, 423, 448, 463-464, 477, 495, 502, 504, 511-512, 588, 589-590, 591, 616, 630, 637, 641-642, 655
Underwood, Susanna Mary	95	M	A: 108	D: 54, 55
Vail, Nellie K. L.	807	M	D: 45	L: 138-139
Valentine, Harrison	427	D	C: 42-43, 80-81, 132-133	G: 545, 557-558, 566, 592-593, 601, 640, 648, 650, 653; H: 13, 15, 38, 55, 56, 71, 86, 113-116, 118-119, 130, 139, 154, 155-156, 157, 194-195, 212, 213, 220-221, 223, 252-255, 358-359
Vallerly/Vallely, John	374	D	B: 785-786	G: 329, 346, 352, 366; H: 536, 555; I: 32, 33, 47, 54-58, 78, 144-146, 162
Van Patton, Charles C.	860	D	D: 100	L: 581-582, 606, 607, 640; M: 118, 139-140, 159-160, 230, 242-243, 305, 365-366, 367, 457-460
Vassar, Benjamin	1042	M	D: 289	O: 444, 466, 473
Vassar, Benjamin D.	998	D	D: 243	O: 106, 118-119, 144, 444, 445, 462, 482, 507
Vassar, Jacob	1042	M	D: 289	O: 444, 466, 473
Vaughn, Bertha J.	1028	M	D: 275	O: 379-380
Vaughn, Spencer C.	1028	M	D: 275	O: 379-380
Vaughn, William S.	1028	M	D: 275	O: 379-380
Veal, William	470	D	C: 138-139	H: 236, 259, 269, 289, 425, 447, 448-449, 479, 481-483, 507-508, 593-594; J: 389, 407, 426-427, 583-585
Vestal, Solomon D.	177	D	B: 161-162, 291-292	E: 247, 253, 272, 274, 286, 301, 448, 463-465, 468-469
Vierra/Vieira, Joseph	933	D	D: 173	M: 429, 452
Von Quitzow, Albert Georg Carl	985	D	D: 230	O: 28, 74, 96, 100
Vreeland, Squires/Squire	361	D	B: 759-760	G: 162, 168, 204, 238-239, 254-255, 259, 273, 280, 299-300, 328, 335-336
Wade, John F.	938	D	D: 178	M: 482, 526; N: 329-330; O: 284
Walker, Nathaniel	355	M	B: 745-746	G: 121-122, 151, 612, 626
Walker, Samuel H.	708	D	C: 674-675	J: 578, 590
Walker, Silas	523	D	C: 254-255, 602-603	H: 566, 595; I: 1, 2, 22-23, 37-38, 73, 165, 179-180, 224-225, 499, 514-515, 541-542; J: 359, 370-378, 394-397, 555-556

Name	File #	Type	Fee Book & Register	Minute Book
Walker, W. N.	942	D	D: 186	N: 163-164, 178, 240-241, 289-290, 564, 587, 590, 599, 616, 631-632; O: 6, 73, 95-96
Warner, Philemon	762	D	C: 794-795	K: 296, 315-317, 440; L: 229-230, 247, 323, 324, 338-343
Washer, Bridget	828	D	D: 66	L: 294, 319-320, 349, 366, 635-636; M: 25-27
Washer, Catherine	766	D	D: 2	K: 313-314, 335, 343
Washer, Johanna M./A.	936	M	D: 176	M: 393-394, 501-502; N: 487-488, 513, 537-538; O: 476-477
Watson, William	445	D	C: 84-85	H: 62-63, 72, 305, 361-364, 439, 440, 554, 563, 587-588; I: 15, 38-40
Watts, Samuel	91	D	A: 103-104	D: 36, 39, 49, 64, 72, 234, 239, 247, 250-251, 274, 277, 300-301, 356
Webb, Henry	798	D	D: 34	L: 49, 62, 88, 284, 305; M: 57, 80, 117, 126-127, 277, 301, 310
Weeks, Parker E.	899	D	D: 139	M: 255-256, 285-287
Weir, James	410	D	C: 8-9	G: 428, 439, 443, 461, 496, 518
Weise, Charles	524	M	C: 256-257	H: 567
Weise, Eliza	524	M	C: 256-257	H: 567
Weise, Frederick	524	M	C: 256-257	H: 567
Weise, Henrietta	524	M	C: 256-257	H: 567
Weise, Henry	524	M	C: 256-257	H: 567
Weisinger, George	257	D	B: 499-500	F: 333, 343, 351, 429, 439-440, 519-520, 545, 552, 562-563
Wells, James L.	676	D	C: 610-611	J: 403-404, 443-444; K: 55, 90-92
Wesel, John	981	D	D: 226	N: 614, 632; O: 1, 9, 279, 287-289
West, Adalaide	62	M	A: 76; B: 259-260, 297-298	B: 216-217; D: 224; E: 438-440
West, Carlos	62	M	A: 76; B: 259-260, 297-298, 331-332	B: 216-217; D: 224; E: 420-421, 438-440, 455, 459, 460, 471-474, 481, 494, 509, 519, 529-530, 533, 550-551; F: 200, 217, 358, G: 153-154
West, Eddie	937	M	D: 177	M: 431; O: 96, 113, 144-145, 146-147
West, Geneveive	62	M	A: 76; B: 259-260, 297-298, 333-334	B: 216-217; D: 224; E: 420-421, 438-440, 455, 459, 460, 471-474, 481, 494, 509, 519, 529-530, 533, 550-551; F: 358-359, 413-414

Name	File #	Type	Fee Book & Register	Minute Book
West, Guadalupe	62	M	A: 76; B: 259-260, 297-298	B: 216-217; D: 224; E: 438-440
West, Guillermo/William	62	M	A: 76; B: 259-260, 297-298, 439-440	B: 216-217; D: 224; E: 420-421, 438-440, 455, 459, 460, 471-474, 481, 494, 509, 519, 550-551; F: 200, 203, 204, 206, 207, 218, 357; G: 154
West, Juan	62	M	A: 76; B: 259-260, 297-298, 329-330	B: 216-217; D: 224; E: 420-421, 438-440, 455, 459, 460, 471-474, 481, 494, 509, 519, 529-530, 533, 550-551; F: 405
West, Marcus/Marcos	62	M	A: 76; B: 259-260, 297-298	B: 216-217; D: 224; E: 438-440
West, Maria del Carmel	62	M	A: 76; B: 259-260, 297-298, 335-336	B: 216-217; D: 224; E: 420-421, 438-440, 460, 471-474, 481, 494, 509, 519, 529-530, 533, 550-551, 359; G: 153
West, Nellie	937	M	D: 177	M: 431; O: 96, 113, 144-145, 146-147
West, Samuel J.	553	D	C: 328-329	I: 163, 173-174, 215, 377, 396, 426-428, 451-452, 466-468; L: 96, 111-112, 130, 132; M: 239-240, 269, 298-301, 438
West, William Mark	62	D	A: 76	B: 76, 106, 178, 390, 396, 397-398, 405
Weymouth, Minnie C.	1018	M	D: 265	O: 315, 316
Whitaker, Peter	405	D	B: 845-846	G: 370, 375, 397, 407, 415, 460, 465, 468-469; H: 31, 39, 45, 46, 161, 163-164, 187-189, 533, 539-541; J: 264
White, Bynam	214	D	B: 337-338, 403-404	E: 544, 546, 554, 600, 608-609; F: 129, 132, 154, 165-166
White, Charles L.	771	D	D: 7	K: 336-337, 378, 386, 387-388, 416; L: 52, 64-65, 140-141, 261, 287-288, 345-348, 444-445
White, James	121	D	A: 136	D: 219
White, Maggie	771	M		L: 307-308, 344-345, 447
White, Wilson	265	D	B: 531-532, 651-652	F: 416-417, 423-424, 432, 462, 514, 525, 530-531, 702, 720, 728-733; G: 7-8, 33-34
Whitlock, James M.	880	D	D: 119	M: 103, 120-121, 143-144, 168-169
Whitman, Lillian/Lillie	456	M	C: 106-107	H: 121, 133

Name	File #	Type	Fee Book & Register	Minute Book
Widdows, Louis	714	D	C: 688-689	J: 620
Wieberts, G. J.	974	D	D: 218	N: 541, 552-553, 572; O: 80-81, 141, 164-166
Wiese, Carl Johannes	812	D	D: 50	L: 153-154, 184, 189-190, 194, 424-425, 517-518, 578-579, 611, 620-621; M: 507-508
Wiley, Hugh	156	D	B: 57-58, 179-180	E: 86, 102, 106, 166, 279, 287-289
Wilkins, Charles P.	261	D	B: 511-512	F: 356, 361, 365, 420-421, 437, 438, 456, 466-467, 469, 472-473, 478, 479-480, 650, 654, 666-667
Wilkins, Henrietta C.	439	M	C: 68-69	H: 30, 104, 105, 143, 171, 197, 199-201, 222-223
Wilkins, Maria S.	439	M	C: 68-69	H: 30, 104, 105, 143, 171, 197, 199-201, 222-223
Wilkins, William	439	M	C: 68-69	H: 30, 104, 105, 143, 171, 197, 199-201, 222-223
Williams, A. A. C.	466	D	C: 128-129	H: 217, 226, 230, 231, 246-248, 256-258; I: 360, 368-369
Williams, James	219	D	B: 357-358	E: 611, 624; F: 3-4, 198, 202, 212-213, 250, 267, 286
Williams, James H.	752	D	C: 770-771	K: 225, 236-237, 238, 255-256, 351-353, 359, 399
Williams, John (alias Scottie)	378	D	B: 791-792	G: 282, 288
Wilson, Albert C.	935	M	D: 175	M: 413, 418, 463-464
Wilson, Celia A.	935	M	D: 175	M: 413, 418, 463-464
Wilson, Gaston	935	M	D: 175	M: 413, 418, 463-464
Wilson, George B.	310	D	B: 639-640	F: 665, 670, 675, 676; G: 116, 135, 136, 142, 154-156
Wilson, George B.	935	M	D: 175	M: 413, 418, 463-464
Wilson, Isaac E.	935	M	D: 175	M: 413, 418, 463-464
Wilson, John G.	779	D	D: 15	K: 418-419, 445-446, 462; L: 7-8, 34-35, 97-98, 120-121, 150, 242-243, 309, 330-332
Wilson, Johnson	437	D	C: 64-65	G: 648, 656; H: 30
Wilson, Leland	935	M	D: 175	M: 413, 418, 463-464

Name	File #	Type	Fee Book & Register	Minute Book
Wilson, Mary E.	934	D	D: 174	M: 447, 486-487, 501, 579, 590-591; N: 347-348, 366-367, 422-426, 499, 519-521, 563-564, 583-584, 588; O: 64, 105-106, 134, 135, 152, 167-169, 179-180, 223
Wilson, William H.	833	D	D: 71	L: 364-365, 380-381, 403-405; M: 60-61, 75-79
Winkler, John Jacob	873	I	D: 113	M: 104, 134, 148, 634-635; N: 38-40
Winn, Helen Augusta	131	M	A: 143; B: 209-210	E: 314
Winn, Jacob	131	D	A: 143; B: 31-32	D: 283, 293, 295, 311, 342, 369; E: 1, 46, 544, 545, 570, 581, 604-605
Winn, Lydia Frances	131	M	A: 143; B: 209-210	E: 314
Wiseman, Ella	377	M	B: 791-792	G: 216; O: 261-262, 282-283, 291
Wiseman, Susan	377	M	B: 791-792	G: 216
Witt, Andrew S.	792	D	D: 28	L: 25-26, 53, 58-59, 68-69, 78-79, 113-114, 140, 151, 160-161, 249-250, 252, 273-274, 279-280, 282-284, 306-307, 321-323, 329-330
Witt, Charlotte	955	D	D: 199	N: 292, 325-327, 331, 339-341, 426-427, 476, 522, 530, 532-533; O: 76, 88-89, 99, 126, 131-133, 355
Witt, J. G. William	958	M	D: 202	N: 338, 516, 563, 609-610; O: 78, 90-92, 112
Wolf/Wolfe, George W.	282	D	B: 569-570	F: 503, 506
Woods, James	551	D	C: 322-323	I: 151, 178-179; J: 232-233
Woods, Sarah F.	328	D	B: 685-686	F: 781, 785, 786
Woodworth, Parmenas Newton	1003	D	D: 248	O: 122, 153, 154, 375-376
Wright, Amelia A.	582	M	C: 398-399, 434-435	I: 397-398, 412-413; L: 596; M: 58, 111-113, 312-313, 330; N: 418, 440, 488-489, 506-507, 510-511, 515, 516-517, 529-530, 558, 578, 587, 589, 599, 607, 633; O: 6, 24-25, 52-53, 102-103
Wright, James A.	582	M	C: 398-399, 434-435	I: 397-398, 412-413; L: 596; M: 58, 111-113, 312-313, 330; N: 418, 440, 488-489, 506-507, 510-511, 515, 516-517, 529-530, 558, 578, 587, 589, 599, 607, 633; O: 6, 24-25, 52-53, 102-103

Name	File #	Type	Fee Book & Register	Minute Book
Wright, John A.	582	M	C: 398-399, 434-435	I: 397-398, 412-413; L: 596; M: 58, 111-113, 312-313, 330; N: 418, 440, 488-489, 506-507, 510-511, 515, 516-517, 558, 578, 587, 589, 599, 607, 633; O: 6, 24-25, 52-53, 102-103
Wright, Sampson	353	D	B: 741-742	G: 122, 149-150, 152, 159, 161, 196, 200; J: 27-29, 73-78, 79
Wright, Sarah E.	582	M	C: 398-399, 434-435	I: 397-398, 412-413; L: 596; M: 58, 111-113, 312-313, 330; N: 418, 440, 488-489, 506-507, 510-511, 515, 516-517, 558, 578, 587, 589, 599, 607, 633; O: 6, 24-25, 52-53, 102-103
Youle, Adam W.	939	D	D: 179	M: 563, 600-601, 622; N: 439-440, 554-555, 572-575, 596, 608-609; O: 4-5, 29, 94, 109-110, 127-128, 184, 209, 215-216, 230, 250, 251-252, 306-308, 311-314, 327, 520
Young, Hiram	663	D	C: 572-573; D: 99	J: 279, 307-308, 338-339, 412, 444-445, 452, 503-504; L: 7, 23-25, 326, 393, 394-395, 432-433, 494-496, 579, 590, 603; M: 113, 177-178, 235-236, 252-253, 278; N: 190-191, 209-214
Young, Sarah	682	D	C: 622-623	J: 431, 448-449; L: 433-434, 497-498, 603-604; M: 113-114, 145-148; N: 189-190, 214-217
Zboinski, Wladislaw	187	D	B: 217-218	E: 322, 331, 365, 387